OBJECT RELATIONS
IN SEVERE TRAUMA

OBJECT RELATIONS IN SEVERE TRAUMA

Psychotherapy of the Sexually Abused Child

STEPHEN PRIOR, PH.D., PSY.D.

JASON ARONSON INC.
Northvale, New Jersey
London

Production Editor: Elaine Lindenblatt

This book was set in 11 pt. New Aster by Alpha Graphics of Pittsfield, New Hampshire, and printed and bound by Book-mart Press of North Bergen, New Jersey.

Library of Congress Cataloging-in-Publication Data

Prior, Stephen.
    Object relations in severe trauma : psychotherapy
    of the sexually abused child / by Stephen Prior.
        p.   cm.
    Includes bibliographical references and index.
    ISBN 1-56821-554-1 (alk. paper)
        1. Sexually abused children—Rehabilitation.   2. Sexually abused
    children—Mental health.   3. Sexually abused children—Case studies.
    4. Object relations (Psychoanalysis)   I. Title.
    RJ507.S49P75   1996
    618.92'85836—dc20   95-32752

Manufactured in the United States of America. Jason Aronson Inc. offers books and cassettes. For information and catalog write to Jason Aronson Inc., 230 Livingston Street, Northvale, New Jersey 07647.

CONTENTS

PREFACE

This book outlines an object relational theory of the consequences of the sexual traumatization of children. It is based on the intensive psychotherapeutic treatment of seriously disturbed boys who had suffered multiple forms of neglect and abuse. To understand the suffering of these children and to create forms of treatment suited to them, I found that I had to develop theory as I went along, for there were no existing conceptualizations that explained the distress of these children or their treatment. Using object relations theory, I have attempted to characterize the ways in which neglect and abuse distort fundamental needs and psychic structures in the child.

What I present is clinical theory. By this I mean theory in which conceptualization and therapeutic practice are integrated in such a way that each explains and elaborates the other. The ideas and methods evolved together, and their joint presentation illuminates more, I believe, than one without the other. The case material is presented in some detail, to reveal the nature of the treatment process and the fundamental transference issues. The theory is nonetheless quite comprehensive. Based in part on the work of W. R. D. Fairbairn, Bernhard Berliner, and Rudolf Ekstein, it analyzes the psychological response to trauma in terms of the repetition of abusive patterns of relationship, identification with the aggressor, self-blame, and the seeking of object contact through sexuality or violence. This scope makes the theory applicable to a variety of treatment situations, such as the psychotherapy of adults who were abused as children. The overall perspective may be of value in other contexts as well, such as group and family treatment, milieu therapy, case management, and forensics.

As the integration of the concepts and methods described in this book took shape, it began to reveal why both psychodynamic and trauma-oriented theories have had difficulty conceptualizing and treating the psychological consequences of overt trauma. Psychodynamic theory has seemed unable to give a substantive causal role to overt events and relationships and has had difficulty conceptualizing the impact of abuse. Trauma theories have focused on external events to such an extent that the scope and depth of psychic injury contingent on psychological trauma is often not fully appreciated or conceptualized. Articulation of the difficulties within existing theories clarifies the proposals I have made and will, I hope, lead to further advances in the treatment of those who have suffered interpersonal trauma.

I have attempted to synthesize these various considerations in order to present a coherent perspective on sexual traumatization in children and its treatment. Theory, practice, and metapsychological reflection must, I believe, evolve together—in part because we know so little in each domain. I hope that this book weaves these strands together in such a way that greater clarity is brought to each area. I also hope that my efforts might inspire others to attempt this kind of integrative venture.

ACKNOWLEDGMENTS

There are many people who helped either directly or indirectly with this book and in the clinical experiences that led to it. Deborah Crossman helped greatly with editing and preparing the text for publication. I would like to thank Beth Parsons, Rachelle Goodfriend, Justin Newmark, Rheta Keylor, and Schuyler Hoffman for their encouragement, comments, and criticisms throughout its many versions. Fred Meisel was invaluable in helping me understand the inner world of the seriously disturbed child. I thank Barry Minsky for his assistance (and insistence) regarding the role of underlying fears of annihilation. My work in general, particularly this book, could not be what it is without Paul Russell, who taught me so much about trauma and the treatment process. My deepest appreciation goes to my wife, Patricia, for her understanding, insight, and encouragement through the lengthy evolution of this work. I thank these people, and unmentioned others, for what they have so generously given me. Without these relationships, this creative effort could not have taken place.

1

INTRODUCTION

Over the past fifteen years, the prevalence and significance of childhood sexual abuse has been increasingly recognized (Browne and Finkelhor 1986, Emslie and Rosenfeld 1983, Finkelhor 1979, 1987, Herman 1981, Sgroi 1982, Summit and Kryso 1978). The role of such abuse in the development of various forms of adult emotional distress has been confirmed clinically and epidemiologically (e.g., Briere 1989, Carmen et al. 1984, Goodwin 1990, Goodwin et al. 1990, Herman et al. 1989, Kluft 1984, 1985, Putnam et al. 1986, Schetky 1990, Zanarini et al. 1989). Increased recognition of the psychological consequences of sexual abuse has been part of a broader recognition of the role that trauma plays in the development of serious emotional distress, adaptational difficulties, and psychopathology (Coons 1986, Eth and Pynoos 1985, Kelmpe and Helfer 1968, Smith

1978, Terr 1991, Ulman and Brothers 1988, van der Kolk 1987). The rediscovery of trauma appears, in turn, to be part of a greater recognition of the impact of real events, persons, and relationships on emotional development (Miller 1981, 1983). A wide variety of perspectives, theories, and practical approaches devoted to trauma and its treatment inform the clinical landscape in a way unimaginable ten or fifteen years ago. This rediscovery (or reconceptualization) of trauma is, perhaps, the central new feature in contemporary clinical thought, and it may represent an important shift in the paradigm of psychotherapeutic theory and practice.

Despite increased awareness of sexual traumatization and the development of new theories and specialized modes of treatment, relatively little has been written for the practicing clinician who deals with childhood sexual victimization in the context of long-term, dynamically oriented individual psychotherapy. This situation is particularly clear (and unfortunate) in the case of child victims of sexual abuse, and even more so in the case of male child victims of sexual assault.

It is also of concern that there is remarkably little literature on the treatment of sexually abused children who, because of the abuse or additional factors—such as early neglect—suffer from serious emotional disorders. Much of the literature on the treatment of sexually traumatized children appears to address the problems and therapy of more intact children, who have developed some degree of psychological integration prior to traumatization. For many children, however, sexual victimization is but one process in a lifelong pattern of neglect and injury. Because of this history of both acute and chronic trauma, these children suffer serious forms of psychic distress. Sexual abuse and its consequences are so thoroughly interwoven with the consequences of neglect, other traumas, and defenses against all of these that understanding any one aspect requires understanding all the others. Therapy for sexual traumatization must necessarily be integrated into the comprehensive treatment of the child and his or her broader emotional suffering.

We have, then, no paradigm theory for the understanding and treatment of seriously traumatized, disturbed children. There is no agreed-upon model of conceptual understanding and therapeutic practice that most clinicians would adhere to, and that would form a framework of shared assumptions, practices, and interpretive ideas. Indeed, there do not even seem to be contenders for the title of current paradigm theory. One suspects that the many clinicians who work with such children are struggling to find their way, with little to guide them and certainly no comprehensive model with which to work.

I hope to address these multiple gaps in our knowledge by providing a detailed and theoretically informed view of the dynamics and treatment of seriously disturbed, traumatized boys. This theory attempts to go beyond description of the symptomatic effects of sexual abuse, toward an explanation of why sexual traumatization produces certain central effects and not others, why it so profoundly affects the child, how it distorts the dynamics and structure of the child's psyche, and how sexual traumatization can be understood in relation to neglect and the child's underlying relational needs. Many of the existing theories that deal with trauma fail, I believe, to offer even provisional answers

to these questions and, as a result, fail to offer intellec-
tually satisfying or clinically useful perspectives.

When I began the treatments described in this book
(in the mid-1980s), the absence of a theory of trauma
that could be the basis of clinical practice was even
more apparent. The significance of overt traumas such
as sexual abuse in the development of psychological distress was just beginning to make inroads into theory and
practice. At that time, now more than a decade ago,
it was manifestly clear that there was no theory that
adequately dealt with children who had suffered pervasive neglect and abuse. There was no theory that
integrated an understanding of the depths of their emotional pathology with an understanding of the role that
overt trauma and abusive relationships played in generating this pathology. The psychodynamic literature
that dealt with seriously disturbed children described
the internally disorganized, traumatized children in my
care and offered important insights into the treatment
process. This perspective failed, however, to describe
the manifest role that overt trauma played in the lives
of most of these children. It likewise failed to articulate certain key dynamics, such as these children's
deeply held belief that they caused and deserved the
abuse, a characteristic noted by many observers. The
data and initial theories in the trauma literature, while
amply demonstrating the reality of sexual abuse and the
seriousness of its consequences, failed to characterize
the internal states of these children and to articulate the
depth of disorder that overt trauma had caused. This
dichotomy of dynamic theory without trauma and
trauma theory without depth has unfortunately seemed

to continue to the present day, despite the obvious and pressing need for some kind of synthesis.

Lacking a theory that could speak to both trauma and dynamics, I sought to develop a more complete view of these children, their suffering, and their treatment. I attempted to create a perspective that could incorporate an awareness of the depths of psychic disorder that analytic theory provides with an understanding of the causal role and unique dynamics generated by overt trauma. To create this more integrated view, I worked on four fronts at once: study of the clinical data and the therapeutic process, study of the trauma literature and psychodynamic perspectives on trauma, reflection on the difficulties psychodynamic theories have with the concept of overt trauma, and the development of a relational theory of the consequences of sexual trauma. These four strands of inquiry are presented in this book. Viewed from one perspective, it is a detailed study of the psychotherapeutic treatment of three quite disturbed boys. Viewed from another perspective, this book tries to say something of considerable generality about object relations, anxiety, and trauma. In another vein, what is portrayed here is a painful exploration of the nature and power of sexual abuse. Viewed from yet another point of view, this work is an examination of the inability of established psychodynamic theory to integrate a useful concept of overt trauma and the failure of current trauma theories to provide a useful perspective on the inner life and psychotherapy of the abused child. Each strand of inquiry is necessarily incomplete. My goal has been to draw out in each perspective that which illuminates something about sexually abused children and about the other three themes. I have aimed not at a comprehensive review of each part but at the development of an integrated view that provides a coherent and useful portrait of seriously disturbed, traumatized children and their treatment.

The theory I propose has considerable generality, in that it analyzes the damage of sexual abuse in terms of the damage done to the child's conception of self, other, and the possibilities of human relationship. I propose that there are four pivotal factors: the repetition of abusive relational patterns, identification with the aggressor, self-blame, and the seeking of object contact through sexual or violent means. These factors are understood as deeply entrenched defenses against annihilation anxiety. As the theory began to take shape, I realized that it bore a strong resemblance to those of W. R. D. Fairbairn and Bernhard Berliner. Their efforts probably exercised an organizing effect on my thoughts, and they deserve due credit. To be made relevant to current clinical practice, their views require theoretical and clinical elaboration, which I have tried to provide. Otto Kernberg's work on unmetabolized object relations offers a useful theory for understanding the damage done to the structure of the child's psyche. Attachment theory elucidates important points in clear and succinct ways, and this theory is presented as well.

While the theory I present has considerable range of application, there should be no illusion about the scope of the clinical experiences from which this theory grew. A great many cases were under my care, but almost all of them were boys, and almost all of these were about latency age. The general theory takes its root in these circumscribed beginnings. However broad may be the ultimate conclusions, the theory surely bears the mark of its concrete origins, as do most psychodynamic theories. It is almost surely true that someone attempting the same integrative task from the standpoint of therapeutic work with traumatized girls would discover clinical information and theoretical perspectives different from (but not alien to) mine.[1] Those working with children less disturbed than the ones I knew would, no doubt, find different perspectives as well. Clinicians whose basic conceptual orientations are different from mine would likely find a different but related landscape. This is part of the inherently perspectival nature of clinical theory. My goal was not and could not have been to develop a general theory of trauma—the kind of thing that might turn out to be so general as to be uninteresting and imprecise. I set out to find a theory that would explain what I was observing and experiencing in the treatments with the children I knew. What was striking, and I think important, was how this seemingly localized theory suddenly seemed to reveal something of broader significance, even while bearing the marks of its practical origin.

---

1. Because all of the treatment cases discussed involve boys, and because the theory has particular relevance to boys who have been abused, I have used the masculine pronoun *he* throughout most of the text. The theoretical ideas and therapeutic perspectives I develop are, however, relevant to the treatment of girls and women as well, as I have found in my clinical practice. The theory I present enables us to conceptualize some of the overt differences and the underlying similarities between the typical responses of boys and girls to severe sexual trauma. Further clinical explication and theory construction about these complicated and important matters is obviously necessary.

If I have in some measure integrated an object relations theory with an understanding of overt trauma, a step has been taken toward an important larger task, the development of *the psychodynamics of trauma.* By this I mean a theory that would reveal how unconscious, relatively universal, internal needs and structures of the human psyche interact with injurious events, persons, and relationships to create distinctive forms of emotional and relational distress. As I pursued my own efforts in this direction, I found that other clinicians had tried to do the same thing, to incorporate a more realistic view of trauma into psychodynamic theory and thereby to create a more accurate, complete, and helpful understanding of trauma and emotional disturbance in childhood. Sandor Ferenczi was the first; his work is still relevant to the current situation. Several integrative efforts, all by clinicians, are described in this book.

My goal has been similar to theirs, to develop a theory not only diagnostically correct but clinically useful as well. Therapeutic practice required a new theory, and my hope was always that the theory would in turn illuminate the clinical process. The theory I propose is intended not just as an abstract model of object relations but as a theory of treatment. The therapies I was engaged in, and the theory that evolved out of them, suggested new perspectives for understanding the treatment process and virtually demanded new modes of engagement with my child patients. In this book, I have attempted to articulate these shifts of perspective and action. In particular, I have tried to describe the need for the therapist to actively interpret the child's relational dilemmas, the need to bring the split-off parts of the self (the "bad self") into the treatment, and the importance of articulating, and in some measure meeting, the child's underlying relational needs. Some of these principles were anticipated by Rudolf Ekstein and his colleagues (see Ekstein 1966), and I owe a considerable debt to their work. I believe, however, that these ideas can now be better understood through the theory and clinical examples presented here.

In order that the theoretical ideas and technical suggestions may be fully understood, I present the inpatient treatment of a seriously disturbed, seriously traumatized boy that lasted four and a half years. This case study also reveals how severe trauma and consequent emotional illness can, under proper circumstances, be successfully treated. I have attempted to describe in some detail what is often lacking in child therapy presentations—namely, the nature of the transferential dynamics and their interpretation in the process of cure.

I have specifically avoided a large set of issues, much discussed nowadays. Considerable attention has been given to Freud's rejection of his earlier seduction theory in favor of a theory of wish and fantasy and to the effects that this conceptual revolution had on later analytic theory and practice. It is now often asserted (e.g., Herman 1992, Masson 1984) that this shift, important perhaps in the development of psychoanalytic thought, was fundamentally wrong, and that it led to serious problems of theory and practice. It is argued, and not without merit, that analytic theory failed to conceptualize the impact of overt trauma generally, and sexual abuse specifically, and that analytic practice often failed to address such issues effectively in clinical practice. I shall not, however, review the historic and social sig-

nificance of analytic theory's apparent failure to integrate a useful concept of overt trauma. Important as
these matters may be, attention to them will not generate the new clinical theories that we need. Recognition
that sexual abuse is common and injurious does not
provide an understanding of the effects of trauma or a
model of treatment. The awareness that we need new
perspectives if we are to understand trauma and its
consequences does not create that perspective. At this
time there can be little argument that sexual traumatization of children does take place (along with other
forms of traumatization) and that the effects of real
traumatization are generally worse than those of the
fantasized. What is important now is the actual development of new theories of trauma. We need to know
what the psychological effects of overt traumatization
are and how to treat people who have experienced it.
The theory I have developed is a partial answer to these
questions.

It is, however, worthwhile to examine why psychodynamic theories have had such difficulty integrating a robust notion of overt trauma. To show how
this occurs, I shall explicate how two influential, traditional perspectives on the origins of serious emotional
disorders in childhood not only avoid the subject of
trauma but actually *preclude* the utilization of a useful
concept of overt relational trauma. Because of this,
these theories fail to come to terms with important features of the distress and treatment of seriously disturbed, traumatized children. I also hope to provide
some insight into the theoretical reasons why it has
been difficult for psychodynamic theory generally to
provide a compelling theory of overt trauma. What I

find interesting is, in a sense, *the resistance in the traditional theory itself to the concept of trauma.* Understanding this resistance reveals, I believe, something of importance in how psychodynamic theory would need to change if it is to become a psychodynamics of trauma.

One may notice that I have not defined the concept of trauma at the start. I certainly rely on the basic Freudian notion that an event is traumatic if it stimulates thoughts or affects so disruptive that the psyche is unable to integrate the stimulus event and the psychological disruption that ensues. In this view, trauma occurs when the psyche is overwhelmed (Freud 1920). Most intriguingly, Freud ties this state of being overwhelmed to the fear of annihilation (1923) and to object loss (1926), but these notions are not fully developed. My point in using a provisional definition of trauma from Freud is specifically not to prejudice the discussion toward an endopsychic, energic, nonrelational view of trauma. The reason Freud's definition continues to be valuable is that we can abstract it from his various problematic theories of mind. We can use the basic definition as a general and imprecise characterization, a definition that alerts us to the scope and depth of trauma. Trying to define trauma further than this without spelling out an entire theory would be unwise or even impossible. What happens to the psyche when it is overwhelmed is what theories of trauma need to explain. Each theory characterizes the traumatic event, the damage to the psyche, the defensive mobilization, and the long-term consequences in different terms. Because all the theories contain the term *trauma*, one might think they are all talking about the same thing. Surely, one might say, they are all about trauma. But each theory of trauma gives new or different significance to the concept. The meaning comes out of the theory as a whole, what it reveals and articulates about overwhelming injury and the psyche. Thus, each theory ultimately defines "trauma" in its own particular way. Trauma in ego psychology inevitably involves damage to the organizing and functional capacities of the ego. In the theory I devise, trauma is understood as damaging the capacity to relate to others, producing specific relational dynamics, and evoking annihilation anxiety. Because the theory defines the concept, we must allow the initial definition to be imprecise.

In the history of psychodynamic theory there is a powerful precedent of looking first at the more disturbed cases and then seeing what they reveal about the less disturbed, and then about all of us and human nature. Part of what is still so shocking and difficult for people to accept about Freud and Freudian theory is that it is not a theory of psychopathology but a theory of normalcy. We are all disturbed. Freud's theory is actually a theory of trauma, a fact obscured these days: The developmentally normal events of childhood—our prolonged dependence on parents, the vicissitudes of our natural wishes, and the recalcitrance of reality— truly overwhelm every one of us and require those defenses and distortions we call neurosis. The disturbed are not some separate class, distinct from and less than the rest of us. The conflicts and forces that beset the overtly disturbed beset us all. Severe pathology reveals a general truth. The theoretical view described in this book offers particular insight into the lives of traumatized, seriously disturbed children. The application to adults who were abused as children will be apparent as the central ideas are developed. But if this theory is truly a good one, and truly a theory with some reach and generality, it should reveal something about human suffering generally. My belief is that certain dynamics, so powerfully seen in the cases I present—attachment to bad objects, self-blame, perversion, and annihilation anxiety—reveal something of importance about basic human anxieties and defenses, about the fabric of suffering in all of our lives, and about the possibilities of realistic transformation.

2

TRAUMA AND TRAGEDY

We are all now aware that there are many children who suffer extensive traumatization at the hands of their parents or other adults, children who in their short lives suffer neglect, emotional exploitation, physical violence, or sexual abuse. But while this general fact may be known, the details of their lives and the extent of their psychic disarray may not, hidden from view by many things, including our understandable wish not to know. What *does* happen when a child is horribly abused? How can we grapple with this reality and begin to understand and then to help? Two representative cases that all too painfully reveal the nature of abuse in childhood and the damage that it does to the very core of the child's self are presented in this chapter.

These are horrible stories. In a literal sense, they could not be worse. But that is part of the clinical vocation—to see, to witness, to take the suffering as a starting point. The clinical journey can only begin with what is.

JOEY

Joey, age 8, had the scruffy, dirty, irritated look common to children who have suffered significant neglect and who, as a result, have had to fend for themselves from an early age. Joey had undergone several psychiatric hospitalizations and residential placements before coming to the inpatient facility where I worked. He never seemed happy and was typically on edge. He was often angry about seemingly small disappointments or affronts. Joey was unable to interact successfully with peers in any setting, being selfish, provocative, and physically violent. He tried to come across as tough and independent, but he was actually lonely and needy. He never seemed to derive much lasting comfort from the kind attention of adults. He fell into states of rage, assaultiveness, and agitation nearly every day. His behavior often led to physical restraint by staff. This, in turn, provoked more agitation and violence, almost surely because the physical restraint replicated various abusive experiences we knew he had undergone. Often, the only thing that calmed him was short-term pharmacological intervention. Joey denied any major problems in life and would not discuss his history or the particulars of his behavior. In therapy, he intensely and persistently played out dramas of physical and psychological abuse: his characters were either being tricked or hit or doing this to me. Joey was deeply attached to me as his therapist. If I was even a minute late, he would fall apart in despair and anger. Yet, there were few expressions of warmth between us in the months we worked together, despite the felt bond between us. Abusive play absorbed all of our time, and Joey seemed reluctant to express positive feelings too overtly. Sharing a few cookies at the end of a session was the closest and quietest thing he would allow. I never felt that I was doing enough for him, even though we met three times a week, and we often saw each other in the residential unit.

Joey's mother was well-known to the state's social service agency before his birth, because of her neglect of his older sister. Joey's father was never a factor in Joey's life, having spent nearly half of his own life in adolescent and adult correctional facilities. When Joey's mother was six months pregnant with him, she attempted suicide by swallowing household cleaners. When Joey was 10 months old, he was removed from his mother's care because of her alcoholism and negligent parenting. From age 10 to 14 months, Joey lived with his maternal grandparents, until it was discovered that he had cigarette burns on his buttocks and anus. Joey was then placed in foster care for approximately four years. In this home, he was repeatedly abused, physically and sexually, by his foster father and foster brother. He witnessed his sister being sexually abused by his foster father and brother. They also taught Joey to kill animals. After removal from this family, Joey smeared his feces, set fires, drank from a toilet, and tortured animals.

When evaluated, shortly after removal from this grotesque environment at the age of 6, he was found to be quite disturbed and significantly regressed. He could relate to adults for the most part in literally infantile ways—being fed, having physical contact, and receiving constant attention. In one diagnostic interview, he volunteered that his favorite food was lobster. He then drew one and asked the examiner to eat it. Next he became very concerned that this lobster was eating the man from the inside. Joey said that the only way to get rid of it would be through defecation, adding that if the man did this, it would be important to stand back quickly from the toilet so that his genitals would be safe from the snapping claws.

After this evaluation, Joey received one and a half years of residential treatment, which helped him in a variety of ways. He was able to attach emotionally to his therapist and other adults, he dealt with some of the issues of loss in his life, and he was no longer so regressed and disorganized. He was able to use both language and play to communicate about important feelings. His full-scale IQ was found to be 94. Unfortunately, as he made overall progress, he was reunited with his mother, despite the fact that her visits produced severe regression and flashbacks of sexual abuse by his foster father. He eventually became involved in sexual activity with other boys and subsequently became suicidal. He was then transferred to my hospital for treatment.

Given this dreadful history, one could say that Joey was actually doing rather well. In a safe and contained setting, he was not psychotic and quite capable of genuine interpersonal attachments and emotional growth. He did not have the pervasive fluidity of thought, instability of defenses, or identity diffusion that often afflict the seriously disturbed children one sees in inpatient settings. Still, he was a deeply troubled child, filled with chronic tension and unintegrated anger, catastrophically reactive to loss of any sort. He frequently relived traumatic events and could regress into states of disorganized distress, irritability, and violence.

FRED

Fred, age 9, had a remarkable ability for going into my office, finding the one thing that had special personal value for me, and destroying it while telling me what a piece of junk it was. If I got exasperated, he would say, much too cloyingly, "You don't like me anymore." If I got angry, he would immediately yell, "Child abuse! Child abuse!" He began one session with me by asserting that I was a homosexual. We eventually began to talk about AIDS, another concern of his. He told me that he had heard AIDS could be spread via bodily fluids. When we finished the discussion and our time was up, he spit directly into my eye. Fred was not very well liked by adults, but there was a basic and consistent way in which he was emotionally reachable. He was universally disliked by peers for provoking others to violence or other trouble and then tattling. Although I could feel angry at Fred, I quite liked him. I think he knew that I could tolerate his sadomasochistic modes of engagement and could understand the eroticized and aggressive play he liked so much.

Fred was sent to the institution where I worked when he could no longer be treated in the psychiatric facility closer to his home. His chronic and unmanageable assaultiveness had been too much for this less contained setting. Fred's involvement with therapeutic institutions began eight months earlier, when he threat-

ened to stab himself in the eye and kill himself with a
butcher knife. Brief inpatient treatments had done little
for him. Throughout the transitions from home to hos-
pitals and back, he had been fortunate enough to have
a very dedicated outpatient therapist who had been with
him for one and a half years.

Fred was a profoundly anxious and overtly fragmented boy when he began therapy with me. His attention would jump from one thing to another with amazing rapidity, though testing revealed that he did not
suffer from a true attention deficit. His IQ was in the
average range. His associations were driven, frantic,
and quite revealing. He could be doing one thing, and
then suddenly grind his pelvis into the back of a chair
and say something like, "Oh baby, give it to me in the
dick!" And then, a few seconds later, he would be sad
and ask when his mother might be coming. Next, he
might engage in some fantasy story about a great
superhero who "can do everything and can change into
anything in the universe." Fred would literally career
around the room as he went from interest to interest.
He spoke in much the same way as he acted. He had an
elaborate range of yells, shrieks, squeaks, and cries. His
voice and whole manner of being would shift as he went
from feeling to feeling, interest to interest. He would
often construct codes that were something of a callig-
raphy, connecting written symbols with spoken words
and feelings. This construction of private languages
conveyed, among other things, his strong (and accurate)
perception that his feelings were not understood by
others and that people had been seriously out of touch
with his needs. One of his lists was comprised of the
following phrases: "Hi. Good-bye. I will miss you.
Scared. Frustrated. Angry. Kiss me. I want to go home.

Let's attack. Let's capture. Let's shoot everyone except the queen." But once one of these sets of phrases had been created, he would lurch to another activity and forget all about it. After ten months of treatment, he was able to list his five major problems, which he dictated to himself through me: "You don't like yourself. You flip out when you're frustrated. You love to destroy. You think about sex when you feel close to someone. You're afraid your anger will kill your mother."

Fred's mother had, in her teens, married a rather violent man who physically attacked her and then Fred. She clearly cared about Fred, but her own background and psychological difficulties had made her concern ineffective. Her parenting skills were focused around practical matters. While well meaning, she had trouble tuning in empathically to what Fred's needs actually were. While it was known that Fred's father had beaten him, it was also very clear that Fred missed him greatly when the parents divorced and that he still longed for a relationship with him. Fred's comments and associations clearly indicated that he blamed his mother for his father's departure, for allowing his father to beat him, and for apparently preferring his father and brother over him. Fred was angry at both his mother and father for paying so little attention to him that he could be sexually abused by someone outside the family. But he was terrified of anger in any form, believing that his anger or bad behavior would drive his mother away.

Fred was open about having been sexually abused. But he was unable (and perhaps afraid as well) to state what had happened and who had been the original perpetrator. His drawings and behavior conveyed quite convincingly that he had been made to perform fellatio on a man and had been anally penetrated by a man.

After four full months of treatment, Fred played out a starkly realistic story of abuse. We constructed a court-room drama in which two child abusers were on trial. Their crimes had been secretly videotaped. The tape revealed that "Billy" had been "touched in the ass . . . fucked in the dick . . . touched down his pants." His abusers told Billy that if he refused to engage in these activities they would "throw him off the Empire State Building." Furthermore, if he told anyone, they would shoot him. Two sessions later, Fred showed me in graphic detail what had been done to Billy, by making the drawing displayed in Figure 2–1. The lips are heavy because they are "covered with slime." The circle with dots at the crotch is "the asshole"; the dots are "bugs, germs." Figure 2–2 shows all the "germs or bugs" in-side that cause pain, that make it hard and scary for him to go to the bathroom and make him crazy. In another session, Fred said Billy has damage "deep inside. . . . [T]here's something wrong with his heart. . . . [I]t just stops beating. . . . He swallowed a balloon with a tick on it, and the tick is in the center of his heart." Fred demonstrated the interrelatedness of the abuse, his anger, and his confused identifications with aggressive men (good and bad) when he told me how he wanted us to try to kill the tick. This tick at the center of his heart makes his character "confused. . . . [E]very time he gets frustrated he has an attack. The attack is called . . . GI Joe!"

While Joey's and Fred's lives are extreme in their degree of traumatization and consequent psychopathol-ogy, they are sadly typical of the children one can see from multiproblem families, in which physical and sexual abuse are but a part of an even larger pattern of

Figure 2–1

neglect and emotional trauma, in which the child is chronically exposed to the worst manifestations of adult pathology.

What is this suffering, so poignantly expressed by Joey and Fred? How are we to understand and help these children? The attempt to answer these questions takes us on a long and complicated journey, from clinical process to theory and back again.

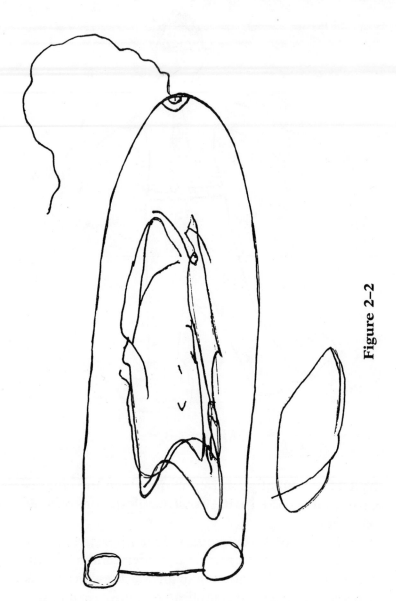

Figure 2-2

3

ON THE
ABSENCE OF AN
ADEQUATE THEORY

THE CONCEPTUAL SETTING

There are three areas of psychological investigation in which we find factual information, partial theories, and clinical perspective about disturbed, traumatized children like Joey and Fred. None of these areas offers a comprehensive portrait, but each provides useful knowledge. The first is the psychodynamic literature on the so-called borderline child. These works deal with a heterogeneous group of seriously disturbed children who bear a strong resemblance to the traumatized youngsters I have described. Studies of borderline children over the past decades provide considerable insight into the psychological distress of the more troubled child and describe the treatment process with great sensitivity. Useful as these studies may be, they are not so widely known outside the circle of psychodynamic practitioners as they should be. In addition, much of this literature predates the recent focus on overt trauma as a distinctive cause of emotional disorder. As we shall see, a variety of theoretical and clinical limitations affect this framework because it does not incorporate overt trauma into its conceptual perspective.

The second source of information is the current empirical research on childhood trauma. As noted in Chapter 1, a voluminous literature about trauma and its consequences has developed over the past fifteen years. Much of it is devoted to the study of adults who were traumatized as children, with significantly less literature available about the actual effects of trauma on children themselves. While this literature captures the factual reality of abuse and its consequences, much of it is strictly empirical research that correlates abuse in its many manifestations with various patterns of emotional and behavioral symptomatology. Theoretical conjecture about the structural or intrapsychic impact of trauma on children has been sparse. There is also remarkably little in this literature about the actual therapy of abused children and little that can be inferred from the empirical generalizations.

There have, fortunately, been a few attempts to synthesize an understanding of emotional and relational dynamics with an awareness of the role of overt trauma. These works are most helpful for understanding and treating children like Joey and Fred. They appear, however, not to be widely known, and their full theoretical and clinical importance seems to have gone unrecognized. This third, small body of literature forms the basis for the larger theory I propose in Chapters 4 and 5.

These three approaches to understanding disturbed and traumatized children will now be reviewed. This review is not exhaustive, for it aims not at completeness but at providing a map of the theoretical and clinical landscape, and initiating a synthesis of major points of view.

BORDERLINE CHILDREN

Since the late 1950s, clinicians have described the behavior, dynamics, and treatment of quite disturbed, disorganized children whose functioning can range from the nearly normal to the frankly psychotic (Ekstein 1966, Fast and Chethik 1972, Geleerd 1958, Pine 1974, 1986, Rosenfeld and Sprince 1963, 1965, Smith et al. 1982). These children show major deficits in ego functioning, object relations, and adaptational capacities, just as Joey and Fred did. Despite its deficiencies in recognizing and articulating the role that overt trauma may play in generating borderline conditions, this literature conceptualizes important features of serious emotional disturbance in children and creates a theoretical perspective useful for understanding the psychological consequences of trauma, whatever the origins.

Synthesizing the major studies of these children, we can create a generalized portrait of the borderline child, a composite or ideal type that captures many of the frequently observed characteristics. No one child will correspond completely to this ideal type, and differences between subtypes will be obscured. The portrait will, nonetheless, reveal much about the children these clinicians have been struggling to understand. This ideal type describes children who are seriously fragmented and overwhelmed, pervasively anxious, and suffering from significant disturbances in all areas of functioning. Their behavior is typically disorganized and impulsive and frequently violent or self-destructive. They have a remarkable lack of signal anxiety: flooded at every turn by primitive thoughts and impulses, they are predisposed to panic and lack most means of self-soothing. Their feelings are typically intense and labile, with anger often predominating. The content of their thoughts, as revealed in spontaneous play, often involves strong components of oral aggression, sadistic anality, and anxious attention to sexual issues. Psychosexual structuralization is quite unstable, with rapid and fluid shifts from oral to anal to genital themes, and with a related fragility and ineffectiveness of defensive capabilities. Particularly at times of stress, their thinking becomes fluid and magical or decays into primary process. Further, their ability to test the reality of their emotionally charged interpretations of the actions and motives of others is strikingly limited. Relationships are often based on object hunger, acute separation anxieties, intense anger, or character defenses against these. Desire for connection and fear of what will occur in relationship create distorted or idiosyncratic forms of relationship and communication. Superego formation is spotty, severe, and punitive. For a host of reasons, their self-esteem is very low. In sum, these children suffer from massive deficits in ego functions and psychic structuralization, however these may be conceptualized. These factors working together create a child whose capacity to master developmentally appropriate tasks is significantly impaired, to say the least.

Helpful as the concept of the borderline child can be, it has gone underappreciated or unnoticed even among child clinicians. The nosological term "borderline disorder of childhood" has not been accepted as a legitimate diagnosis in the standard diagnostic manuals. The reasons for this relative nonacceptance are complex (Shapiro 1983). For one thing, the significant emotional and behavioral differences between various subtypes of the disorder prevent the establishment of definitive diagnostic criteria (Pine 1974). In addition, the concept of a borderline disorder of childhood is thoroughly embedded in psychodynamic theory and practice, and it is not readily amenable to reformulation in the more observational terminology favored by epidemiologists or clinicians working outside a dynamic perspective. There is, for example, no translation of dynamic notions such as "failure of phase dominance" into more observational or theory-neutral terms. Finally, the absence of clear or compelling etiological theory in the borderline child literature is troubling for those who, understandably, want classification schemes to correlate with the various causes of emotional pathology.

Considerable confusion has been generated by the common and erroneous assumption that borderline children are equivalent to borderline adults who happen to be children. This thesis is often assumed or asserted by those who have written about adult borderlines, and even by some who have written about disturbed children. The assumption may derive simply from the shared use of the term *borderline,* or from the shared use of certain theoretical formulations. Whatever the origins of this assumption, there is considerable reason to believe that it is false. Most borderline children are more fluid and chaotic in their thinking and affect than the stably unstable borderline adults (described by Kernberg 1966, Masterson 1972, and Rinsley 1978, 1980, 1985) who utilize splitting to defend against psychological disorganization. Many borderline children appear to be truly borderline psychotic (see Knight 1953), to have entered the fluid and primitive states against which splitting defends. While complete developmental studies are lacking, it appears that, while a few borderline children grow up to be borderline adults, many do not and, instead, suffer from more severe disorders (Greenman et al. 1986, Kestenbaum 1983, Lofgren et al. 1991).

In using the borderline child literature to understand and conceptualize the problems of the sexually traumatized child, we encounter another problem—namely, that the existing literature either does not address etiology or does so in a way that tends to minimize the role of interpersonal trauma significantly. Ekstein (1966), whose work is descriptively vivid and clinically astute, does not address the origins of the borderline child, confessing "our efforts have been clinically rather than genetically oriented" (p. 102). In his rich and insightful clinical descriptions, there is no mention of overt trauma. After suggesting at one point that trauma could play some role, Ekstein concludes that we must understand the borderline child simply as suffering from "defective ego controls" (p. 102). (The impact of parental character is briefly described but not articulated in any general sense.) Other studies of borderline children similarly emphasize ego deficits in their descriptions of the syndrome and focus on constitutional factors in the etiology (Fast and Chethik 1972). The origin (not always acknowledged) of many of the broader theoretical formulations about borderline children appears to lie in the framework developed by Otto Kernberg in the 1960s to understand and treat adult borderlines. If we examine Kernberg's early work, such as "Structural Derivatives of Object Relations" (1966), we see that he hypothesizes that the fundamental source of borderline conditions lies in innate ego deficits, such as weakness in integrative capacities, and in innate overabundance of aggressive drives. As we shall see in detail in Chapter 6, little or no room exists in Kernberg's theory for any notion of trauma.

There is, however, within Rinsley's (1978, 1980, 1985) and Masterson's (1972) elaboration of Kernberg's conceptualizations about adult borderlines, a powerful etiological theory that does incorporate a notion of interpersonal trauma. Derived in part from the work of Margaret Mahler (1971, Mahler et al. 1975), this revised theory states that the disturbed mother recruits her infant or child into her own unintegrated object-relational patterns and demands emotional responses and actions from the child that have nothing to do with the child's developmental or personal needs. Most specifically, the borderline mother is said to interpret the toddler's push toward separation and individuation in terms of her unresolved feelings of abandonment and her own need for a comforting selfobject. As a result, she thwarts the child's drive for independence and autonomy, threatens the child with abandonment, and rewards the child's attention and involvement with her. The child then develops an anxiously compliant pseudopersonality to meet the mother's wishes and to preserve the relationship with her, all the while fearing abandonment or engulfment by the mother's intense and largely oral needs. The child's anger about this untenable situation, in which the child must lose him- or herself in order to have a needed relationship, is typically turned against the self. The theory holds that this relational pathology is particularly injurious during the rapprochement subphase of the separation–individuation process, roughly 16 to 26 months of age. During this phase, the toddler's needs to explore the world away from the mother and to return to her for comfort are both at a maximum. At this same time, the internalized selfstructures that allow for the tolerance of the anxiety of separate and autonomous existence are just in the process of creation and thus are at their most vulnerable (Mahler et al. 1975).

Disruption at this developmental phase is conceptualized as adversely affecting the child in profound and pervasive ways, which Rinsley (1978) identifies as (1) excessive reliance on splitting; (2) confusion of self and other; (3) serious deficits in object constancy; (4) incapacity to mourn; (5) presence of unmetabolized part–object representations and unintegrated, primitive affects; (6) failure of phase-specific (oral-anal-phallic) defensive structure; (7) stunted ego development; and (8) hypertrophied sensitivity to the needs and feelings of others and a consequent development of varieties of psychological compliance (pp. 47–48).

The clinical and theoretical significance of the shift from the early, Kernbergian theory of innate deficits to the now standard theory of interpersonal psychic injury needs to be emphasized. At the heart of the revised theory is a clear and powerful notion of interpersonal trauma, though it is not stated in these terms. In the revised theory, the *real* thoughts, feelings, and actions of the mothering figure are seen as possible causes of significant emotional damage to the child. Whatever the metapsychological beliefs of its proponents may have been, this revised theory opened a door to the psychodynamic study of overt emotional and interpersonal trauma and to the study of the complex relationship between the actions and character of parents and the intrapsychic dynamics of the injured child.[1]

This revised theory of the origin of adult borderlines has had a curious impact on research into borderline disorders of childhood. On one hand, we continue to see the direct importation of the theory to explain borderline conditions in *childhood* (Kernberg 1983, Rinsley 1980). On the other hand, for some it has clearly had no impact at all. Pine's (1986) work continues the emphasis on innate ego deficits and limits the effect of interpersonal trauma to poor maternal ministration and its effect on the stimulus barrier and other ego capacities.

It is, further, no longer obvious that the specific claims of the standard and revised theories of the origin of borderline conditions are correct or that some of the basic concepts (such as separation-individuation)

---

1. The early and revised theories together also appear to have been instrumental in introducing object relations theory into common clinical thought and practice in the United States, in bringing to the fore the study of pre-oedipal conflicts, in opening new forms of dynamic treatment to more seriously disturbed patients, and in initiating the dialogue between clinical theory and parent–child observational studies—not a small series of accomplishments.

are the best for understanding early emotional development or later psychopathology (Lyons-Ruth 1991). Independent of the truth of any specific part of the theory, there is a fundamental limitation in even the revised theory's capacity to conceptualize the effects of interpersonal trauma. In the revised theory, there is one and only one trauma: the psychological use of the infant by the borderline mother during rapprochement to meet her own emotional needs. The pathogenic relationship is conceptualized as operating during a limited time frame and along only the dimension of separation-individuation and no other. No other relationships, dynamics, or behavioral traumas are discussed. I think it is now generally recognized that the concept of interpersonal trauma must cover more overt dimensions of interactional and relational dysfunction than maternal neediness during rapprochement. While the revised theory begins the study of the psychodynamics of trauma, it so strictly limits the range of traumatic events and the conceptual parameters used to understand traumatic injury that it is in need of substantial revision and augmentation.

Despite its fundamental limitation, the clinical power of the theory and the significance of the clinical data should not be overlooked. While the current tide of psychological theory is very much oriented toward overt forms of trauma, the significance of less overt but profoundly damaging relationships in the first two years of life still remains to be fully incorporated into the study and treatment of disturbed children. The eight categories of psychic injury so carefully presented by Rinsley (1978) capture many of the dynamics one sees in these children—dynamics that are essential to grasp if one is to work in a long-term clinical context with them. As we shall see in both the theoretical and clinical material to follow, a general theory of trauma may not be possible until overt abuse and its consequences are understood in relation to the states of disorganization that can result from deficits or pathogenic emotional dynamics in the early parent–child relationship.

If we attempt, then, to summarize the application of the borderline child literature to the study of traumatized children, we find a complicated picture indeed. On the one hand, this literature gives an excellent portrait of the internal disorganization and primitive needs often seen in sexually traumatized children. The consistency of the clinical portrait, the sophistication of the theoretical understanding, and the usefulness of the therapeutic recommendations are undeniable. On the other hand, the theory fails to address the role that overt trauma in general and sexual abuse in particular often appear to play in the etiology of borderline conditions. In both the child and adult studies, there is uncertainty and confusion about the causes of these disorders. Kernberg's and Pine's theories are heavily loaded toward the innate and constitutional factors and actually tend to prevent the incorporation of overt trauma as a cause. (This point is demonstrated in detail in Chapter 6.) The revised adult theory recognizes the effect of real actions and relationships on the child during the rapprochement phase of the separation–individuation process, but unfortunately it constrains the concept of interpersonal trauma to a highly restricted range of dynamics. These restrictions on the role of overt trauma tend to prevent recognition of pivotal intrapsychic and relational dynamics that are essential for understanding and treating traumatized children.

THE CHANGING CONCEPTUAL FRAMEWORK

A paradigm shift in psychological theory appears to be taking place at this time. Trauma, in a broad and general sense, has now become a central phenomenon that all clinical theories must describe and explain in some way. Simultaneously, trauma has become a central etiological factor in new or revised theories of the nature and origin of emotional distress. Reconceptualization of psychopathology in the light of increased understanding of childhood trauma has had a powerful effect on clinical theory and practice with adults and has stimulated vigorous debate inside and outside the field.

The transformation in theory is most evident in the reconceptualization of the concept of borderline personality in adults. Empirical evidence and theory now point to the important role that childhood abuse plays in the origin of this range of disorders (Coons 1986, Goodwin et al. 1990, Herman et al. 1989, van der Kolk 1987, Zanarini et al. 1989). In the more complete reconceptualizations, the borderline personality diagnosis is supplanted by post-traumatic stress disorder, thus changing not only the causal theory but the basic typology as well.

The full recognition of trauma and its effects cannot help but transform clinical practice in a variety of ways (Herman 1981, Perry et al. 1990, Saunders and Arnold 1993). In some broad but largely unarticulated manner, this has already begun. Exactly how these changes in theory and practice transform psycho-dynamic therapy and theory is far from clear. Attempts by several psychodynamic clinicians (Davies and Frawley 1992, Levine 1990, Shengold 1989) to integrate a more robust notion of trauma into adult clinical practice demonstrate the complexity of the conceptual and therapeutic issues involved in integrating a new concept of trauma into a psychodynamic perspective.

While the psychotherapeutic treatment of emotionally troubled adults has undergone significant theoretical and clinical revision, less attention has been given to the effects of trauma on children themselves. Much of the existing literature on the impact of childhood trauma deals with correlations between such trauma and *adult* psychopathology. The connections between childhood trauma and *childhood* pathology have been less extensively studied. No new theories of childhood distress have been presented, nor has any older theory been challenged, perhaps for the very reason that there is no consensual paradigm theory of childhood psychopathology to critique.

The empirical literature regarding the consequences of trauma in children does document the serious injury done by inappropriate sexual contact with adults. In these works, as in the more familiar literature on adults, sexual traumatization is shown to be correlated with a broad range of behavioral, cognitive, and emotional dysfunctions. Valuable as the empirical studies have been in revealing the prevalence of childhood trauma and the power of its effects, they are ultimately of limited clinical usefulness. As Finkelhor and Browne (1985) point out, summarizing this literature would merely generate a giant list of possible outcomes of sexual trauma. We are presented with a mosaic of features of mental life and behavior that have little apparent relationship. There is no theory that would explain how the data are related, what the facts mean, or what the nature of psychological trauma actually is. Empirical studies of trauma typically choose not to discuss the nature of the child's experience, internal processing, or psychological structures in any form, perhaps because these intrapsychic dimensions are considered less accessible to empirical verification. While demonstrating the tangible effects of real abuse, the focus on observable symptoms unfortunately tends to obscure the depth and severity of the long-term, psychological consequences of trauma that can be better formulated in theoretical terms. If psychodynamic theories have been resistant to the reality of overt traumatization, empirical studies have been resistant to the formulation of theory and to the need to come to grips with the internal experience of the abused child.

The empirical research has produced a few attempts at conceptualizing the effects of overt trauma on children, such as those created by Finkelhor and Browne (1985), Goodwin and colleagues (1990), and Terr (1991). Terr's research, for example, into a wide range of traumatic experiences (not all of them interpersonal) reveals that four characteristics are of singular importance in diagnosing and understanding traumatized children. They are the presence of "(1) strongly visualized or otherwise repeatedly perceived memories, (2) repetitive behavior, (3) trauma-specific fears, and (4) changed attitudes about people, aspects of life, and the future" (p. 12). In recurrent trauma, she reports, the surprise and shock of an unpredictable and unexpected event give way to anticipatory dread of repeated traumatization. The constant dread of inescapable events requires "massive attempts to protect and to preserve the self . . . massive denial, repression, dissociation, self-anesthesia, self-hypnosis, identification with the aggressor, and aggression turned against the self" (p. 15). Rage, absence of feeling, and despair are the typical feelings experienced by these children.

Finkelhor and Browne (1985) attempt to understand the trauma of childhood sexual abuse in terms of "four trauma causing factors, or what we will call *traumogenic dynamics*—traumatic sexualization, betrayal, powerlessness, and stigmatization" (p. 530). These four factors are understood as causes of the damage to the child but also as general categories for conceptualizing the effects of sexual abuse. They are "useful for organizing and categorizing our understanding of the effect of sexual abuse" (p. 533).

The generalizations derived by Terr and by Finkelhor and Browne appear to be attempts to define fundamental categories or factors into which most of the empirical data will fit. We could view this as a step toward defining a post-traumatic stress syndrome for children. As noted earlier, the delineation of new syndromes can reshape our vision of our patients in powerful ways. The recognition that disturbed children may indeed be victims of trauma and that much of their manifest symptomatology may be post-traumatic phenomena is an essential step in the development of a deeper understanding of their distress and improved methods of treatment.

While syndrome definitions do not give us a full portrait of the inner life of the traumatized child, there

are insightful and useful notions within these definitions. For example, we saw that Terr describes how
repeated traumatization forces the child to cope not
only with overwhelming external events but also with
the hopeless dread of inescapable suffering. Dealing
with this chronic helplessness and fear, the child is
driven to take extreme defensive maneuvers in order to
preserve psychic integrity, such as identification with
the aggressor or dissociation. Thus, in Terr's view, part
of the injury of external trauma is that the psyche must
use extreme and self-damaging efforts to protect itself.
Terr's analysis correctly suggests, I believe, that part of
what we mean by trauma is the psyche's attempt to
protect against or heal psychic injury already suffered
or future injury that is feared.

Finkelhor and Browne's theory articulates the way
sexual abuse creates an interwoven fabric of psychological effects: sexualization, stigmatization, betrayal of
trust, and powerlessness operate on, and in, the psyche
to create unique and powerful suffering. For example,
it is not just that relationships with adults are sexualized but that this occurs within a context of betrayal
and powerlessness that makes the experience even more
damaging psychologically. Finkelhor and Browne suggest that sexual abuse is so injurious because of this
combination of interrelated consequences.

Definitions of syndromes are, however, only a partial step toward a satisfactory theory of trauma. Despite
the apparent accuracy of Terr's and Finkelhor and
Browne's categories, the child's experience of trauma
and the nature of the injury to the child's mind still
remain obscure. What abused children feel, how they
make meaning of their experiences, and the conscious

and unconscious processes that shape these experiences are not described. Theoretical attention is largely focused on constellations of symptoms or defenses. Neither theory provides a model of why sexual trauma causes particular patterns of response to occur. Why, for example, does sexual abuse cause such persistent anxiety, sexualization, identification with the aggressor, or chronic repetition in life and memory? Why does sexual abuse cause sexualization rather than a flight from sexuality? The lack of a theory of internal states and the lack of a causal perspective seriously weaken the capacity of these theories to articulate the nature of trauma. The pivotal distinction between the traumatic event, the psyche's initial responses to trauma, and the persistent defensive efforts observable long after the trauma is not developed. The word *trauma* is ambiguously used to refer to an external event and to internal processes of the psyche that persist after the event itself. The empirically based theories blur an important distinction as to whether the many observable symptoms *are* trauma itself or *are evidence of* trauma, which would then have to be understood in a deeper way. Syndrome definitions focus our attention on major patterns that need to be explained by a more comprehensive theory, but they do not provide that explanation.

In a somewhat broader context, it is troubling that many of the empirically based studies and their more theoretical offspring fail to discuss the relationship between overt traumatization and other causes of emotional distress, such as chronic neglect. In focusing so exclusively on overt trauma, they fail to attend to other sources of childhood suffering and do not develop a more comprehensive understanding of child development or psychopathology. How the child experiences and copes with overt traumatization is obviously dependent on the child's earlier experience. Surprisingly, many of the empirical studies and trauma-oriented theories do not adequately discuss interconnections between age, gender, developmental stage (however defined), and trauma. Clearly the same overt traumatic event can have different effects on the child at different stages of development (Eth and Pynoos 1985). It is likewise troubling that so much attention has been focused on overt traumatic events while perhaps equally pathogenic effects of chronic relational pathology are not noted and not conceptualized. Most sexual abuse occurs in the context of relationships that are disturbed and distorted in various ways. The differential effects of the sexual or violent encounters and the pathology of the entire relationship must be discriminated. It seems that this point has not been fully appreciated in some of the research, and it connects to an unfortunate tendency to leave the effect that abuse has on the child's capacity for relationship unconceptualized.

The overall lack of attention to questions of earlier trauma, pathogenic relationship, preexisting emotional conditions, and developmental considerations makes much of the trauma perspective problematically generic: the models offer an understanding of how sexual trauma affects all children. What one often needs in clinical work is an understanding of the *differences* in the ways children come to make sense of trauma and their lives as a whole. Understanding the interaction between overt trauma and its immediate psychological consequences, earlier influences on the child, and characterological defensive operations is essential if we are truly to understand trauma in the child's life. The utility of these generic perspectives for helping us understand and treat more seriously disturbed children, like Joey and Fred, for whom overt sexual abuse is but one of many forms of traumatization or injury they have suffered, is limited indeed.

The shortcomings of empirical theory and the theories that have evolved within some loosely defined trauma perspective become apparent when one looks at the clinical part of the theory. The reluctance to theorize about the child's internal experience tends to vitiate the therapeutic perspectives, rendering them superficial. The child is essentially treated as needing relief from the overt symptoms, through a sort of abreactive treatment in which the facts and feelings around the trauma are discussed with a comforting adult (see Walker and Bolkovatz 1988). The therapist is told to establish trust with the child; to find ways of discussing the memories of actual events; to help the child express feelings of fear, anger, sadness, and grief; to counteract the child's sense of responsibility and shame; and to assist in the confrontation of abusers or the initiation of complaints in the legal system. This mode of treatment seems designed for children for whom trauma has been an intrusion into a life in which there has been some significant degree of stability and order. Helpful as such treatment may be in its proper context, it is impossible and in many respects irrelevant for children like Joey and Fred, for whom trust, relationship, and the capacity to focus on reality have been so shattered. The prescribed treatment is well beyond their psychological level of organization. Further, this focal attention to the reality of trauma is seriously incomplete in terms of what these severely traumatized, disorganized children need from therapy. Their internal disorganization and relational pathology require therapy of greater substance and attention to unconscious dynamics. The disorganizing effects of trauma and the reliving of traumatic relationships, often in the therapy itself, are in large measure not addressed by a "memory of reality" approach.

Some works in this genre (James 1989, Jones 1986) do describe underlying beliefs and feelings that are seen as ultimate causes of the child's manifest behavior. Particular emphasis is placed on the child's feelings of responsibility or guilt for the abuse he or she has suffered. The need to address such assumptions vigorously in the child's treatment is strongly asserted, and some helpful technical suggestions regarding these matters are described. But even these works fail to develop any kind of theoretical conception of the nature of the psychological damage done to the child, and thus they fail to illuminate how such techniques are to be embedded into a comprehensive understanding of the child's internal conflicts and the treatment as a whole. These works only indirectly discuss the unconscious repetition of traumatic relational patterns in the child's current life and do not discuss transferential issues and their role in the treatment process. The most that is said about the therapeutic relationship is that the child should be reassured and made to feel safe with the therapist. In sum, the therapeutic suggestions developed in the trauma literature fail to address essential elements of the treatment process, especially for the more seriously disturbed child.

ATTEMPTS AT INTEGRATION

What appears to be needed for the understanding and treatment of seriously traumatized, disturbed children is a perspective that can articulate the effects of serious interpersonal trauma on the basic structures and dynamics of the child's mind. The nature of these effects and the child's defensive efforts in relation to them must be described and explained. Such an understanding would constitute what I have termed the psychodynamics of trauma.

A number of authors have, in one fashion or another, attempted to do this very thing. Their efforts, as we shall shortly see, are surprisingly comprehensive, theoretically sophisticated, and clinically insightful. They have not, however, been fully appreciated. They are not, to my knowledge, utilized or even mentioned in the vast array of current studies of traumatized children. Nor do they seem to have had much impact on psychodynamic theory and practice. Why works of such quality should be largely ignored is a troubling question. It may be that their accomplishments have simply not been understood. The role of trauma in dynamic theory and the role of internal dynamics in trauma theory are almost by definition outside the theoretical purview of the adherents. Further, these creative and synthetic works do not embed their clinical or theoretical understandings within a larger historic or metapsychological frame that might call attention to the significance of their more specific contributions. And finally, none of these works integrates basic theoretical concepts, dynamic and etiological hypotheses, clinical data, technique, and historic perspective into a comprehensive model.

Ferenczi's (1933) theory, while not developed in detail, is nonetheless rich and compelling. He begins with the idea that sexual traumatization creates a distinctive and serious form of anxiety that requires an equally distinctive and serious mode of psychic self-protection. He states, emphasizing the entire passage himself, "[T] *he weak and undeveloped personality* [of the child] *reacts to sudden unpleasure not by defence, but by anxiety-ridden identification and introjection of the menacing person or aggressor*" (p. 163). Because of this identification and because the normal need for tenderness and care is now stronger than ever, the abused child attends to the wishes of the perpetrator and eventually to the needs of others generally. The child feels immense shame and guilt, but at the same time he or she feels innocent. This confusion, and the disorientation caused by the replacement of love with sexuality, create a fundamental doubt about reality testing. The child typically feels that self-protection is not deserved. Even more deeply, he or she does not understand what self-protection *is*. Sexual abuse disorients the child's fundamental assumption of deserving love, care, and attention from parents and adults generally. The confusion of tongues arises when the child thinks that the love he or she needs so much consists in the sexual passion the abuser offers. The child comes to believe deeply that the way to have this love is to "speak" the language of passion the perpetrator demands. To maintain order in a world where love somehow means abuse, where the innocent are guilty, and where those you trust are those who hurt, the child's psyche fragments and divides, at times to the point where each fragment "behaves as a separate personality yet does not know of the existence of the others" (p. 165).

These insights remain fresh, powerful, and useful to this day. Their truth will be apparent to anyone who has worked with sexually traumatized children. We shall see these ideas demonstrated in the clinical material presented later.

Ferenczi's perspective is, however, deficient in one respect that must be commented on here. His stated view is clearly that an abuser offers the child sexual love instead of the proper love of a parent for a child. As many therapists, researchers, and victims have noted, most abusers in fact offer the child violence or violent sexuality in place of love. They do not give the child sexual love at all but sexual hate. These differences are not lost on the child. The role of hostile and destructive intent within sexual abuse is generally large and powerful. Aggression and responses to it play a significant role in the theory I present later.

The work of A. H. Green (1978, 1983) on the psychopathology of abused children is, in part, an attempt to correct the failure of the borderline child literature to address the role of trauma in the etiology of severe childhood disturbances. Green describes a large class of children and adolescents who, like Joey and Fred, are typically from low socioeconomic backgrounds, who have suffered multiple losses and traumas, and who are seriously disturbed. He then demonstrates, in a broad and general way, the role that trauma plays in the development of these children's disorders. He articulates several pathogenic dynamics that entrap such abused children even after they have received relief from their more acute distress. Unfortunately, Green's work does not seem to have received the recognition it deserves. Green was one of the first to state explicitly that overt trauma can generate specific and persistent dynamics. This important conceptual step has not been widely appreciated.

Green defines abuse as a complex factor, involving physical or psychological assault that conveys destructive adult hostility or abandonment in a context of overall neglect and deprivation. He identifies several severe and pervasive consequences of such abuse. Some are more general, such as overall impairments of ego functioning, high levels of anxiety, defensive distance from others, and powerful responses to separations of any type. Others are more specifically tied to dynamics of trauma, such as the repetition in action or in play of abusive events, the formation of relationships that mimic the abusive ones, and identification with the aggressor as a key mode of defense. Green believes that the central and fundamental consequence of a neglectful, abusive early interpersonal environment is the absence of psychological structuralization. This deficit in psychic structure exposes the child to powerful forms of annihilation anxiety. In addition, children raised in such environments develop intense feelings of guilt and responsibility. According to Green (1978), they "ultimately regard themselves with the same displeasure and contempt that their parents directed toward them. The young children who were repeatedly punished, beaten, and threatened with abandonment assume that it was a consequence of their own behavior, regardless of their actual innocence" (p. 99). This sense of responsibility leads to self-destructive and masochistic behaviors. The theory I present in Chapters 4 and 5 confirms every aspect of Green's theory.

The clinical reports of Juliet Hopkins (1984, 1986) are the most thorough attempts to portray the treatment of seriously disturbed, traumatized children from a psychodynamic standpoint. She has attempted to integrate a psychodynamic understanding of internal life with a recognition of the impact of external trauma on the child psyche. Her works report on longer-term (two years or more) psychotherapy of children who were subjected to various traumas, including serious neglect, exposure to adult pathology, and sexual abuse. Her rich and thoughtful presentations document the internal disorder of such children and the replication of traumatic relationship that occurs in the transference. Many of the principles that Ferenczi and Green describe are amply demonstrated in her work. Since her focus is very much on the clinical process and not theory, the richness of her work cannot be conveyed in summary.

In the case most fully described, Hopkins (1984) tells us of a girl who came to treatment at the age of 6 with rage attacks, transitory psychotic functioning, an overt masculine identification, and a remarkable shoe fetish that included but was not limited to licking the shoes of other patients in the waiting room. This quite troubled little girl, Sylvia, had lost her affectionate but overstimulating father in an auto accident just before treatment began. She came from a household in which she was exposed to considerable turmoil, impulsiveness, anger, and disorder. Both her mother and father had little capacity to parent. Sylvia was beset by intense longings for a good object, often expressed in literally cannibalistic ways that appeared most strikingly when Hopkins took vacation. Sylvia oscillated rapidly between rageful fantasies or acts of violence toward others and intense fears of violation by others. She could deal with her anger and consequent guilt only through strenuous efforts at splitting, eloquently expressed by Sylvia herself when she said, "That was the other Sylvia that hit you, not me. I smacked *her* in the eye" (p. 81). Despite having suffered a variety of forms of emotional, physical, and sexual abuse, Sylvia could not think of her parents as being responsible or as harboring hostile feelings toward her, as was the case.

Sylvia's treatment involved exploration of fantasy, affect, and play in the service of bringing about greater psychic order and revealing the causes of her quite troubled state. Every reconstruction of a trauma from the clinical material and its interpretation to Sylvia led to psychological growth and integration. (Sylvia's mother later confirmed the reality of events surmised in the interpretations.) Growth and integration were not, however, without their costs. Interpretation of sexual abuse by her father did lead to the disappearance of the shoe fetish and the delusional masculine identification. But the partial working through of these interwoven issues exposed Sylvia to acute feelings of physical and psychological vulnerability, which made her at times depressed and at times angry at Hopkins for removing her primary defense against memories of violation and feelings of vulnerability.

Hopkins (1984) sees no contradiction in using analytic theory to inform the treatment of those who have been overtly traumatized. She states:

The analytic literature suggests that the therapist's ability to reconstruct external events is of particular importance when the patient has taken psychotic flight from reality or when important adults in the patient's life have put a taboo on knowing. In both these conditions, which applied to Sylvia, the therapist risks colluding with the patient's defences if he treats the traumatic events as fantasies. He may also risk repeating the behavior of the original traumatogenic adult, for, as Balint points out, it is common for an adult who has traumatized a child to behave afterwards as though the child had simply imagined it. [p. 85]

As the treatment was ended prematurely after two years, at the mother's insistence, Hopkins was becoming increasingly aware of how difficult it was for Sylvia to recognize the defects and malevolence of her parents and to work through a completely erroneous sense of responsibility for all the painful and confusing events that had befallen her. In the cases and theoretical material I shall discuss, many of Hopkins's clinical observations are confirmed, including the primitive disorganization and extreme defenses that early abuse can create, the role of identification with the aggressor as a pivotal defense, the role of guilt and responsibility, the seeking of object contact through perverse means, and the significance of the therapeutic relationship in the treatment process.

4

RELATIONAL DILEMMAS OF ABUSED CHILDREN

If the existing theoretical and clinical perspectives take us to only a partial and incomplete understanding of serious disturbance in traumatized children, how then shall we understand them? How are we to understand boys like Joey and Fred, victims of neglect and abuse, children both tormented and tormenting? If we synthesize the clinical data, the empirical studies, the psychodynamic portrait of the borderline child, and the integrative attempts of Green and others, we find, I believe, that four factors constitute the basic psychological dynamics of these children:

1. The relentless reliving of abusive relationships, either as victim or as perpetrator
2. The reliance on identification with the aggressor as a basic mode of psychological defense

3. The unshakable conviction of being the cause of the abuse, deserving the abuse, and being utterly bad
4. The seeking of object contact through physical violence, sexuality, or some combination of the two.

Let us examine each of these in turn, in the lives of Joey and Fred.

RELENTLESS RELIVING OF VICTIM–VICTIMIZER EXPERIENCES

Traumatized children, like Joey and Fred, can be observed to repeat abusive patterns in every relationship, either as a victim or as a perpetrator. These children suffer again at the hands of others or in some fashion torment others. There are, for them, no other modes or means of relating with others. The domain of benign and comforting relationships is small at best; without treatment, it may be nonexistent. We can see these patterns on a macroscopic level, in the way that many abused children grow up to become abusers themselves, become victims in abusive relationships, or treat themselves abusively through masochistic attitudes and actions. One sees these patterns just as clearly in their current relationships and interactions. Fred, who spit in my eye while we discussed AIDS, was constantly inviting rejection and punishment in skillful and provocative ways, including physical assault. But the emotional pain he felt when rejected or insulted by anyone was a palpable reminder of the extent of his vulnerability. Joey was similarly aggressive and violent and responded to any limit or constraint as though he were being abused once again.

These patterns of victim-victimizer often become painfully transparent in the child's play, in which there is constant alternation between perpetrator and victim roles. Joey loved playing out stories in which he would trick me or in which I would try to trick him. His favorite was "Pizza Delivery." In this often repeated drama, I would pretend to be a pizza delivery boy. Beneath the pizza, I would carry a gun or a knife and would try to distract Joey with the pizza so that I could wound or kill him. He delighted in being able to protect himself and derived a sense of mastery from being able to protect himself in play as he had not been able to in life. But this protective play was not sufficient. He would quickly move us to stories in which I was the victim of his attacks. In one variant, he would get behind me and have me describe going to sleep after a stressful day. Just as I reached the point of sleep, he would scream full force into my ear.

Fred made the dilemma of being a victim or a perpetrator perfectly clear in the first months of our work. We frequently played out stories of abandoned and abused boys who were trying to get home. He often had me play the role of a boy trying to get home using complex and indecipherable maps. Fred explained that I would be tortured and "put to sleep" at every place I stayed on the way. Description of these torments gave way to brutal demonstrations, with Fred coming at me with a rubber knife and throwing it at my face. He insisted that I resist him violently. I was openly reluctant to be too aggressive toward him, but he made it perfectly clear that there was no alternative. He stated unequivocally, "You will have to kill me, or I will kill you." Relationship would be truly impossible, for either I would be his victim, or he would be mine.

IDENTIFICATION WITH THE AGGRESSOR

The hopeless dilemma of being either a victim or an abuser is interwoven with the psychic problems of identification with the aggressor. Beset by immense feelings of vulnerability, a child will use identification with the aggressor as an internal antidote to feelings of fear or weakness, and he or she may also use this identification actively as a means of preventing perceived revictimization. This dynamic is particularly strong in boys who have been sexually abused by men. Boys typically reason unconsciously that if one is sexually assaulted by a man, then one must be a homosexual or a woman. Identification with the male aggressor is then needed as a defense not only against weakness and vulnerability in general but against implicit feminization.

When, however, a child identifies with the aggressor to deal with the vulnerability and powerlessness he so deeply feels, various psychological dilemmas arise. On some level, the child must recognize that he has become, and in a sense has chosen to become, a very bad person indeed. The child may have the comforting illusion of being strong and powerful, but at the significant cost of being aggressive, violent, and bad in his heart and actions. Further, when the child identifies with the aggressor, he must take out on himself every anger and judgment he feels toward the abuser. If the child feels the abuser should be tortured and killed for what he has done, so now the child must treat himself the same way. In the play of children like Joey and Fred, one can repeatedly observe a sequence moving from vulnerability to identification with the aggressor to guilt. In identifying with the aggressor, the child has only appeared to win a victory. Instead, he is caught in a larger and unresolvable dilemma: If he is weak, he is vulnerable all over again. If he is strong through identification with the aggressor, he will do to others what has been done to him and so deserves the most horrible punishments.[1]

These intense feelings of guilt for aggressive action can explain otherwise perplexing behaviors. When Joey, for example, was punished by milieu staff, he would

---

1. The nature of identification with the aggressor in abused girls is a complicated issue that deserves detailed clinical investigation and theoretical elaboration. While overt identification and resultant guilt are certainly more common and more overt in boys, Hopkins's work (1984) makes clear that overt identification with the aggressor as a defense against vulnerability is quite possible in girls as well. I suspect that identification with the aggressor is often supplanted in girls by identification with the aggressor's view of the child. This causes profound self-hatred and disregard. The girl may even come to believe that protection comes by way of masochistic surrender. Since boys who have been abused are often subject to these same dynamics, it would perhaps be more correct to say that the balance, or relative weight, of identification with the aggressor and identification with the aggressor's view of the self tends to be different in boys and girls. Grave anxieties about vulnerability, the nature of the self, and aggression are the result in either case. A helpful way to conceptualize these matters theoretically is presented in Chapter 5.

usually protest vehemently that it was entirely unfair—
no doubt reflecting his underlying conviction that his
abuse had been unfair. He would fly into a rage and
assault staff members, accusing them of the most
vicious behavior and heartless attitudes. After being
calmed—through talk, physical restraint, or pharmacological intervention—Joey would approach staff quite
apologetically. They would usually forgive him and be
tender and comforting. At that moment, Joey would do
something quite self-endangering, such as sticking his
fingers into an electric socket. The meaning of this sequence becomes readily apparent when one understands the role of identification with the aggressor and
primitive guilt in the child's mind: punished, Joey felt
unjustly blamed and attacked. Reliving the physical
abuse he had suffered earlier in his life, he became terrified and angry, and retaliated. But by attacking the
staff, he became, in his own eyes, a vengeful and abusive person. When he saw that these parent figures were
good, he saw himself as bad for attacking them and
nearly driving them away. He was guilty of attacking
what is good and spoiling his chances of a healing relationship. Hence he must try to destroy the bad within
himself, both as punishment and in the hope of becoming good.[2]

---

2. Protest against past or current abuse may evoke in the child's
mind the fear that such assertive action is tantamount to aggression against the abuser. Distinctions between justice and revenge,
legitimate and illegitimate force, and legal punishment and abuse
may be lost because the child's sense of what is just has been so
violated and because the child's capacity to separate legal fact from
vengeful fantasy may be diminished. The child may truly fear that

While the seriously abused child may wish, out of guilt and anxiety, to destroy or dispose of the identification with the aggressor that protects him against vulnerability, he knows unconsciously that this aggressive identity is part of who he is and cannot be discarded without great cost. The need to identify with the aggressor, guilt about doing so, and a deeper understanding that integration of the aggressive identity is problematic were all made clear by Joey in his very first therapy session. He played out a story based on a monstrous, destructive character whose job it was to protect a little baby. This monster was rageful on the inside but literally made of cold stone on the outside, and as a result it was inviolable. Joey suggested that we saw the two parts in half and discard the angry interior because its fiery rage destroyed everyone in its path, even the baby. When I conveyed that this would weaken and ultimately dehumanize the remaining part of the monster, Joey introduced a mother who fed the baby and the now integrated monster. This appearance of a nurturant and caring figure signaled the correctness of my interpretation and revealed the pivotal importance for the abused child of bringing together the split-off and dis-

---

if he pursues justice, he will have become as destructive as the abuser. Such feelings are an important and overlooked cause of the difficulty many traumatized children, especially the more disturbed, have in confronting their abusers. Naively pressuring a child to confront a perpetrator can create considerable guilt and anxiety. One needs to reassure the child not only that he will be protected from the abuser but also that the perpetrator will have a fair trial, will have a lawyer on his side, and will be protected from cruel and unusual punishments, even if these are wished for.

avowed parts of the self, even the monstrous parts, into some kind of working whole.

PERVERSE OBJECT CONTACT

When a child is chronically abused by adults who get their relational needs met in sexually perverse or aggressive ways, he or she can readily come to believe that the only way to have a relationship is through violence, sexuality, or some combination of the two. This is what Ferenczi (1933) meant by "the confusion of tongues": the child ultimately wants to speak the language of tenderness and comfort. But, through abuse, this language has been supplanted by one of "passion"—sexualized contact. Twice Joey became involved in sexual activity with peers, and each incident occurred in the context of loss and loneliness—one involving a friend's leaving the hospital, the other involving his foster parents' canceling a visit.

The sexually abused child has to contend with feeling that his loving impulses, his desire for relationship and contact with others, bring about what is perverse and violent. It is one thing to believe that one's aggressive feelings injure others or turn relationships bad. It is even worse to believe that one's affiliative desires are ultimately perverse, destructive of relationship, and the cause of one's own abuse. This cruel paradox, that the desire to love and be loved causes violence and perversion, is, I believe, one reason that sexual abuse is so damaging to the child's sense of self and other. The child comes to believe that love destroys.

This confusion of tongues, and the paradox that one's love causes hate, are heightened by the confusing and perverse intentions so common in abusing adults. The underlying emotional needs of the adult perpetrator often have little or nothing to do with love in any form or even sexuality. The abusing adult's real concerns and intentions often have much more to do with power, sadism, or the management of primitive anxieties. These may often have their origin in the abusive childhood of the abusing adult, which is now being reenacted. The "passion" the child meets is rarely the natural sexuality of adults. Adult perpetrators are often deeply confused as to which language they are speaking.

Perverse impulses present the child with further dilemmas: The child fears that if he acts in the aggressive or eroticized ways he now feels impelled to do, good and caring adults will reject him because he is perverse. Fred played out elaborate stories about unlovable characters who were desperate for love and affection but who ruined their chances for relationship through violence or brutal sexuality. Typically, his wretched male character wanted to win the love of the woman character from her husband, but he could not because he was so perverse as to be unlovable. In one story we used dolls based on the wrestling villain "The Iron Sheik" and the hero "Hulk Hogan." The Iron Sheik wanted Hulk Hogan's girlfriend. Hulk Hogan was jealous, but the girl was inclined to be sympathetic. Fred then explained that the Iron Sheik picked his ass and drank his piss and so could never win the love of the woman. I asked how the Sheik got this way, and Fred spoke of himself, saying,

"No one ever loved me, not even my parents." I said, "That is horrible. But why does no one love him?" He said, "He picks his ass." I asked, "Why does he do this?" Fred said, "No one ever fed me." We played out these events with dolls several times. I said it was the worst story I had ever heard. He told me that the Sheik thinks of killing himself. I said, "He thinks no one loves him because he picks his ass. But really, he picks his ass because no one loved him. He has it backward." Fred then played out a story in which the Sheik's death led to rebirth in a happy home with a good father who, not surprisingly, looked just like me.

SELF-BLAME

Neglected and abused children typically believe they caused the losses and assaults they have suffered and believe they deserve them. When Fred's outpatient therapist of one and a half years had to terminate with him, he said to me, "She knew how much I wanted her to stay, but she left anyway." I asked, "Why did she leave?" He replied, "She left because she didn't like me anymore." Joey had an unshakable conviction that his behavior made certain things happen. Despite forceful and repeated explanations of the actual reasons for the scheduling of visits by his foster parents, Joey believed that if he was good, they would come more often, and that they came as infrequently as they did because he was bad. Whenever he did anything wrong in his dorm or at school, he would first protest total innocence but would then take on all responsibility and absolute blame even if others were more culpable.

The intensity of Joey's conviction that he had caused his own abandonment was revealed in our fifty-fifth session. I had announced that our work would be ending because I would be leaving the hospital. He locked me up (in play) for abusing his baby brother. In prison, I was not allowed to talk to anyone. I was lonely. Suddenly, he let me try to call my mother in heaven. He then said, "Your being bad killed her." I yelled, "No!" I explained how awful it was to feel this—it made me feel suicidal. I said, "It wasn't my fault. She wasn't strong enough." Joey ignored this and said she had sent me a last letter. But I was so bad he ripped it up, including "the picture of her face she sent you." Again I was in agony. I was finally allowed to read her letter. I read it as, "Dear Son, I know you think your being bad was what killed me. Well, it wasn't. I just wasn't strong enough. I had lots of problems of my own." Joey listened intently, but then said firmly, "This isn't what it says. It says it is your fault. You were bad. Your being bad killed her."

Evolving from this core sense of self-blame, the child comes to believe that he can evoke rejection or aggression from adults or even that who he is, as a person, is sufficient to cause abandonment or cruelty from adults. The child will then attempt to provoke what for him is the inevitable abandonment; rather than wait for the other shoe to drop, to suffer powerlessly once again, the child will try to turn passive into active by provoking anger and rejection. Abused children are often adept at doing this and can succeed in getting therapists and even whole treatment systems to reject them. The child's core sense of worthlessness and guilt is repeatedly reinforced, making it all the more powerful.

Abused children often develop a powerful sense of their ultimate badness. Many abused children develop a spontaneous conviction that they literally contain a "bad self" that can take possession of them and must therefore be driven out or destroyed. When Joey ceased putting his fingers in electric sockets after being comforted, he began banging his head against a wall instead. He remained largely unresponsive to questions about these acts and simply had to be kept safe. One day the whole pattern occurred just before therapy. On the way to my office, Joey tentatively banged his head against a wall. I stopped him and said (with some exasperation), "What are you trying to do? Bang the badness out? You know, that really doesn't work!" He stopped in his tracks and asked, in a normal but somewhat sad voice, "It really doesn't work?" I assured him, in no uncertain terms, that it did not. After this, he was significantly less self-injurious.

The "bad self" appeared early in my work with Fred. He told me in our fifth week that the only way to rescue the "Good Fred" was to kill off the "Bad Fred," which he wanted me to do in rather eroticized ways. He insisted there was no other way it could be done. I was reluctant to ally with this splitting and self-murder but finally agreed on the grounds he suggested—that he would be totally bad for the rest of his life unless he killed off the Bad Fred. He suggested, "I will cut the evil out of me and out of you, and then we will both be good." (His representations of me and my characters fluctuated rapidly between good and bad, just like his.) To cut out the bad parts, we were supposed to cut our "dicks" off. I expressed serious doubt as to whether this, or any such cutting off, would make us good. He insisted we do it anyway. So we did, and it didn't work at all: we became all bad. Fred then suggested killing himself. He surrendered this idea when I viciously and histrionically said that he should kill himself, that he really was just horrible human garbage. Fred loved this and seemed relieved, but in the end he had his character play out suicide, explaining, "I have a monster inside myself." In the sessions that followed, his despair and suicidal ideation diminished when I pointed out that without the Bad Fred, the Good Fred was weak. Together we then discovered that the Bad Fred had come to power when the Good Fred was small and weak. The kingdom was under attack by powerful and evil forces, and the Bad Fred was the only effective defense against the attack.

POSSESSION

The virtual absence of a conflict-free self, the overwhelming power of identification with the aggressor, and the primitive sense of containing a bad self account for one of the most common and most striking symptoms of disturbed, traumatized children—namely, that they suddenly appear to be truly *possessed* by intense, affectively charged models of interaction that they live out with drivenness and immense pain. One sees again and again how the smallest disappointment, punishment, or loss evokes an intense and complete transformation of the child. They do not simply become angry or upset; rather, they become possessed by terror and rage in quite frightening ways. Children in this state often have immense strength and a nonrelatedness that is absolutely chilling. Traumatized children are often fascinated by (and only occasionally frightened by) movies such as *Nightmare on Elm Street* and its monstrous and indestructible main character, Freddie Krueger; or *Alien,* in which monstrous creatures grow, implanted in normal humans; or *The Exorcist,* in which an outwardly normal girl is possessed by the Devil. The relentless return of the evil characters in such films may express abused children's fear that the perpetrator will find and abuse them again. But the fear, of course, really goes much deeper: The child fears that he will become possessed by the abuser's spirit and become so fully identified with the aggressor that he will act in horrible ways toward others. The abused person fears being abused again *but also fears becoming an abuser. He fears that he will become like the abuser and traumatize others.* This is the fear of possession by the bad object. Possession captures the abused child's belief—often all too accurate—that he will not simply act like his abuser but that he will *become* an abuser, that his entire personality will be taken over by a complete and fully formed evil identity. Abused children's spontaneous belief that they contain a "bad self" is troublingly accurate. In possession by the bad self, the passivity and helplessness of the original abuse by another is reexperienced, except now the child is passive relative to psychic control by an identification. The problem of possession is made all the more difficult when, as in Joey's case, the child acts out his identification with the aggressor. Joey had been cruel toward animals, assaulted other children sexually, and was frequently aggressive. He had thereby "allowed" possession by the bad identity to take place, which created particularly intense feelings of hopelessness and guilt.

If we look again at these four patterns—alternation between victim and victimizer roles, identification with the aggressor and subsequent guilt, self-blame, and the seeking of object contact through perverse or violent means—we see that each is based on a psychological contradiction. It is intolerable to live life as a victim: one is weak and powerless. But it is equally intolerable to live life as the perpetrator, for then one deserves all manner of punishment. It is intolerable to be completely alone and unconnected. But it is equally intolerable to seek relationship through perversion or violence. It is intolerable to be a passive and helpless victim. But it is painful to escape from this helplessness by believing that you caused and deserved abuse. The escape from passivity is achieved by feeling inescapably bad inside. The abused child struggles, then, with what truly are dilemmas, both of logic and of life. The abused child believes:

1. I have two choices in life: to be a victim or a victimizer. Each is unbearable, unlivable.
2. If I am vulnerable, I will live in terror of being abused again. If I identify with the aggressor, I may be safe from retraumatization, but I will have become what I hate most. I will be guilty of doing to others what was done to me, and I will have to take out on myself the rage I feel toward the perpetrator.
3. If I remedy my powerless and passive state by believing I caused and deserved the treatment I received, I have within myself the bad-

ness that causes such horrors and the belief
that I can make these things happen.

4. I cannot bear to exist alone and unconnected
   to others. I desperately need human love and
   contact. But the only way to make real contact with others is through perverse and aggressive ways. My very need for relatedness
   causes me to be a victim or a victimizer.

When the child's life has consisted primarily of neglect
and abuse, there are few, if any, good experiences or
persons to internalize. The child is then forced to internalize the abusive objects in his world. Then the child
is confronted with an ultimate paradox:

5. If I do not internalize the people around me,
   I am empty. But if I do internalize abusive
   objects, I have become, at the very core of my
   self, that which is evil and destructive. Either
   I am nothing or I am bad.

These unsolvable contradictions constitute the basic relational dilemmas of the abused child. From these
basic dilemmas, the child can infer any number of other
dilemmas, equally tormenting. The child may well
begin to believe:

6. I originally thought I was good. But since I
   deserve abuse I am bad. I don't really know
   what I am. I don't really know what is real.
7. I hate the abuse. But since the way to have
   contact with others is through abuse, I want
   what I hate. I truly am perverse.
8. I am enraged about the abuse I have suffered.
   But surely this rage is what caused the abuse.

>And further, people are right to reject or be
>cruel to me now, because I am so rageful.

And thus more and more areas of the child's feelings, actions, and relationships are caught in a desperate web of pain and contradiction.

The living out of these dilemmas constitutes the child's internal life and real relationships. Each contradiction leads to the next, from emptiness and vulnerability to identification with the aggressor, from identification to guilt, and so on. These psychic conflicts absorb the child's life and energy, providing only a piecemeal order, generating intense affects and anxieties, requiring primitive defenses and unstable symptomatic compromises. A coherent self does not emerge, and the child is thrown into panic and disorder.

5

INTERNALIZED MODELS OF RELATIONSHIP

The dilemmas of relationship just described express core conflicts in the lives of seriously disturbed, traumatized children. These fundamental assumptions about self and other cause immense psychic pain, generate significant internal disorder, and prevent psychological integration and sustaining relationships. The interconnected operation of the four basic patterns—reliving, identification with the aggressor, self-blame, and perversion—explains much of the child's behavior, fantasy life, and character development. Let us then take these four basic factors as a starting point, as a basic portrait. What does the apparent truth of this portrait tell us about the mind of the disturbed, abused child?

PSYCHIC STRUCTURE

As was often said of borderline children, seriously traumatized children are generally described as disorganized and labile. But understood in light of the relational dynamics just defined, we can begin to see an
underlying order. Traumatized children are, I suggest,
both organized and disorganized by the psychic contradictions that beset them. Each particular act or feeling has its logic, pattern, and meaning. The child shifts,
as we saw earlier, from one pattern to the next: from
aggression to guilt, from loneliness to longing, from
longing to perversion, from perversion to withdrawal
and loneliness, and so forth. These shifts typically flow
with amazing rapidity and are often disguised through
defensive operations. The child seems disorganized but
is actually being driven from one side of a relational
dilemma to another, or from one dilemma to the next,
in a readily understandable fashion. Each fragment of
behavior is based on a rigid, emotionally charged template of self and other in interaction. These templates
are not well integrated and exist in psychological isolation from one another. It is as if the child has several
predetermined scripts of pivotal interactions with others that are never revised and never edited into one
consistent story. They are often played out with striking clarity in the relationship with the therapist.

Kernberg (1966) describes just such patterns for
borderline adults. He could be speaking of traumatized
and seriously disturbed children when he states:

In these patients there was an alternating expression of
complementary sides of a conflict, such as the acting

out of the impulse at some times and of the specific defensive character formation or counterphobic reactions against that impulse at other times. While the patients were conscious of these severe contradictions in their behavior, they would still alternate between opposite strivings with bland denial of the implications of this contradiction, and they would also show what appeared to be from the outside a striking lack of concern over this "compartmentalization" of their mind. [p. 236]

The fluctuating, intense, and unintegrated patterns of affect, fantasy, behavior, and relationship can be understood, suggests Kernberg, as the manifestation of "'non-metabolized' internalized object relations" (1966, p. 237). Different dynamics, or different sides of the personality, appear as a result of "oscillatory activation" (p. 237) by different stimuli in current relationships.

Understanding traumatized children as suffering from the painful oscillation of relational templates is, I believe, fundamentally correct. The relational dilemmas I have described are examples of unmetabolized object relations, in Kernberg's sense. Because the contradictions cannot be resolved and because the pain and memory of abuse cannot yet be integrated, each dilemma is lived out independently but then pushes the child to the next one. Unintegrated clusters of relational patterns constitute the form of the abused child's psyche, the unstable structure that underlies the fragmented and intense patterns of their lives, feelings, and relationships.

These templates of thought, affect, and action—each complete in itself but unintegrated with the others—

would appear to have their origin in real experiences
of neglect and abuse that have been internalized.
Kernberg (1966), in fact, states that these patterns
become the persistent structural reality of the person
when there has been a "pathological fixation of severely
disturbed, early object relations" (p. 243). Despite this
kind of claim, and despite the consistent use of relational language, Kernberg actually identifies constitutional factors and innate deficits in the child's psyche
as the cause of this pervasive internal disorganization.
This fact, and its effect on the capacity of the theory to
incorporate a useful notion of interpersonal trauma,
will be demonstrated in Chapter 7. In contrast, the
theory I am proposing states quite directly that the internalization of pathological relationships is a fundamental aspect of relational trauma, and as such it is
essential in understanding the nature and consequences
of sexual abuse. A variety of theoretical and clinical
considerations that support this theory are developed
in this chapter and those that follow.

MASOCHISM, PERVERSION, AND THE NEED FOR RELATEDNESS

If the structure of the abused child's psyche is conveyed
in the notion of an unmetabolized object relation, what
can be said about the *content* of the relational dilemmas I have outlined—reliving, identification with the
aggressor, self-blame, and perversion? These four factors have been noted and discussed by clinicians and
theoreticians who have dealt with certain adult emotional disorders. The entire pattern is what Bernhard

Berliner described long ago as "moral masochism" (Berliner 1958). "The masochistic attitude," Berliner states, "is the bid for affection of a hating love object" (p. 41). It originates in "the conflict between the infantile need for being loved and the experience of suffering at the hands of the love object" (p. 41). Though Berliner was writing at a time when the exploration of fantasy and wish were central features of psychotherapeutic practice, he speaks at great length about the *reality* of "the ill-treating parent," who meets the child and the child's love with many forms of "non-love" (p. 43). Masochism, in its essence, involves "the introjection of another person's sadism" (p. 51). Children who have been "traumatized" (Berliner uses this word) in this way continue to look for love through the cruelty of others. Their "experience of hate and ill-treatment is repressed. The child, in its imperative need for love, accepts this hate and ill-treatment as if they were love, and is not conscious of the difference" (p. 44). If the child (or adult) were ever to feel anger about this treatment, he would naturally fear loss of the abusive love object. Loss of the loved object is so intolerable for ill-treated children (because they have had nothing good to internalize) that instead of risking such loss, they will blame themselves for the abuse and treat themselves accordingly. The concern of the child (or adult) throughout all of these manifestations is not, Berliner argues, sexual masochism or the expression of aggressive or erotic impulses. The central motive is the finding of human connectedness on the only terms offered.

It is remarkable that the overtly masochistic attitudes of abused children have rarely been noted as such and that understanding their object relations in this way has not been incorporated into the current clinical and theoretical discussions about trauma and abuse.

In discussing treatment, Berliner (1958) asserts that working through identification with the aggressor is "the most important part of our work" (p. 48). He recommends that the therapist offer a certain measure of genuine gratification in the relationship, so that the patient has, "perhaps for the first time in his life, . . . the experience of a human being who gives him friendly understanding instead of the criticism and punishment to which he has been accustomed" (p. 52).

Another author from an earlier generation who eloquently describes the object relations of abused children but who is not yet fully appreciated in the modern context of trauma studies is W. R. D. Fairbairn. Despite renewed interest in Fairbairn's theories, the application of his work to the treatment of adults abused as children and to abused children themselves is only now just taking place (Davies and Frawley 1992). In "The Repression and Return of Bad Objects," Fairbairn (1952) tells us himself that one of the main clinical sources of his theory was the evaluation of sexually abused children (p. 63). The theory that Fairbairn outlines is remarkably similar to Berliner's, though the theoretical terminology is different. Fairbairn hypothesizes that the fundamental drive of the child is to maintain object contact with some adult in his world, no matter how disturbed the adult or how disturbed the relationship may be. The infant or young child, in Fairbairn's view, shapes his character to conform to the emotional demands imposed by the character and pathology of the parent. This conformation to the parent's character structure serves to maximize relatedness to the needed object. The less available or the more disturbed the parent, the stronger the child's need for relatedness, and hence the stronger the conforming attachment. The child correctly believes that if he fails to comply with the relational possibilities held out by the parent as the only allowable modes of contact, he will be left with no primary relationship at all and will then suffer overwhelming states of isolation and anxiety.

To preserve relatedness to the parents and their painful or peculiar relational demands, and to preserve what amounts to an illusory sense of trust in his interpersonal environment, the child will develop rigid, self-negating beliefs to account for abuse or neglect by the parents. Relatedness to the parent and belief that the parent is good and reliable are so profoundly needed that the child assumes that the parents are good and that their hostile or perverse actions are a direct response to the badness of the child. The child reasons that if only he were to act differently, then his parents would be good and loving. In the child's view of things, the causal and moral responsibility for the painful relationship lies entirely with him (Fairbairn 1952, p. 65).[1]

In taking on (or taking in) all this badness, the child achieves the illusion of living in a good world surrounded by loving parents. But the child then faces a dual dilemma. First, the child subjects himself to all the anger and judgment that he believes the abusive par-

---

1. Incidentally, we can see in this why sexual exploitation by a therapist later in life is so traumatic for a person abused as a child. Such a replication confirms the patient's belief that he or she causes people to be abusive and deserves such treatment as well.

ent (the bad object) deserves. Following from this, all sorts of punishments must be engineered or self-inflicted. Second, the child knows that he has internalized and identified with the bad object and fears that he will be "'possessed'" (Fairbairn 1952, p. 67) by the bad object with which he is so thoroughly identified. This identification with the aggressor is desired (as an antidote to aloneness and vulnerability), is repellant (as terrifying and devouring of the good self), and is punishable (to the degree that it takes hold of the personality). The child cannot live without this complex introject but lives in agonizing conflict with it.

The child will then unconsciously seek out relationships that replicate all the patterns of the original and traumatic relationship, as a way of coping with his internal conflicts and divisions and as a way of maintaining relatedness to others in the only ways he knows. Overtly, the child is driven to repeat the relationship with the abusive parent by recurrent masochistic object choices or by identification with the aggressor. Internally, the child is both aggressor and victim.

ATTACHMENT THEORY'S PERSPECTIVE ON INTERNALIZED OBJECT RELATIONS

The notion of the pathogenic effect of internalized representations of traumatic relationship has received explication and confirmation from recent developments in attachment theory. Attachment theory (Ainsworth 1982, Bretherton 1985, Main and Weston 1981) was first a research paradigm, focusing on the relatively observable facets of early mother–child bonding. Central in the research has been the use of the Ainsworth Strange Situation Test (Ainsworth et al. 1978), in which a mother and young child are observed together, then the child alone, then the child with a stranger, and finally the child reunited with the mother. Observation led to typologies of malattachment. Particular forms of damaged attachment have been correlated with emotional, behavioral, or interpersonal relatedness later in life (Lyons-Ruth et al. 1989, Main and Cassidy 1988). As the theory has evolved, attention has moved from observation of actual interaction to theorizing about the representation of relationship in the child and the parent and about the mechanisms of intergenerational transmission of pathogenic forms of attachment (Main et al. 1985, Sroufe and Fleeson 1986). These concerns have, in turn, intersected with investigations of abuse and trauma. For example, studies have been conducted on the effects loss and trauma have on a mother's capacity to attach to and comfort her child, with resultant difficulties for the child (DeLozier 1982, Lyons-Ruth et al. 1989, Main and Hesse 1990, Parsons 1991).

The theoretical concepts developed in the attempt to explain intergenerational transmission of injurious forms of attachment are remarkably similar to the theory I have developed—internalized object relations and their manifestation in the relational life of the person. As a core theoretical notion, the attachment theorists use the "working model of relationship." This concept derives from the work of John Bowlby (1969, 1973, 1980) and is designed to capture a person's largely unconscious beliefs, assumptions, feelings, and expectations about human relationship. Elaborating on this notion, Zeanah and Zeanah (1989) describe the working model of relationship that infants and children develop as providing:

> internal rules for the direction and organization of memories and attention. [These working models] govern how incoming interpersonal information is attended to and perceived, determine which affects are experienced, select the memories that are evoked, and mediate behavior with others. [Finally, working models] seem to *compel* an individual to recreate experiences congruent with his or her relationship history. [p. 183]

The working model is, then, a template embedded deep within the psyche that provides a set of beliefs, expectations, and feelings about self, other, and the possibilities of relationships. The working model of relationship is an internalized object relationship made operative, mobilizing belief, memory, and affect, in the ongoing life of the person. The working model is the attachment theorist's unconscious, repetition compulsion, and object relationship all rolled up into one concept.

Since a working model consists of correlative conceptions of self, other, and the relationship itself, the working models of the abused child must resemble something like this:

Other: sadistic abuser
Self: vulnerable victim
Relational action: violent abuse
Affect: terror and pain

or

Other: vulnerable victim
Self: sadistic avenger
Relational action: violent abuse
Affect: sadistic glee and guilt[2]

It has often been noted that abused children know how to abuse and that some will grow up to victimize others. Attachment theory provides a unique and conceptually economical explanation of this process. Sroufe and Fleeson (1986) suggest that "abused children learn not only the role of the exploited but the role of the exploiter. . . . Each partner 'knows' all 'parts' of the relationship and each is motivated to recreate the whole in other circumstances, however different the required roles and behaviors might be" (p. 61). Thus, "mistreated children carry forward both the capacities for being mistreated and for mistreating others" (p. 61). The violently abused child does not have two working models, one in which he is a terrorized victim and another in which he is gleefully sadistic. Rather, these are two sides of *one and the same working model*. The intense and effective ways in which abused children can be aggressive toward others are explained as resulting from the same relational model in which the child suffers as a victim. The working model compels the child to be not only a victim in relationship after relationship but also, in other ways or in other relationships, a victimizer. In attachment theory, the development of a masochistic

---

2. These working models are identical to Otto Kernberg's internalized object relational units, which consist of set patterns of affect and action between self and other. I do not believe that the fundamental similarity between attachment theory and Kernberg's views has hitherto been noted.

sense of self-as-victim is at the same time the development of a sadistic sense of self-as-victimizer. This is but an old idea seen from a new point of view—that sadism and masochism are two sides of the same coin. What is replicated in both overt identification with the aggressor and overt masochism is the abusive early relationship.

This notion of working models of sadomasochistic relationship allows us to reconceptualize identification with the aggressor in a useful way. The theory of relational dilemmas I propose places considerable emphasis on the role of identification with the aggressor and thus might appear to have some difficulty articulating the psychological development of the abused girl. While there are important theoretical and clinical factors that remain to be investigated, we can use the notion of working models of relationship to gain a more abstract point of view in which important commonalities in boys' and girls' responses to traumatic abuse can be revealed. Rather than thinking of identification with the aggressor as fundamental for boys and some other process as fundamental for girls, we can think of the abused child, male or female, as developing an abuser–victim dyadic working model. In this view, the child internalizes the abusive relationship itself and identifies with *both* abuser and victim roles. In what is called masochism, the child overtly identifies with the victim role. Covertly, the child identifies with the abuser and abusive role, and will internally abuse him- or herself through blame and self-hatred, believing that he or she is getting exactly the treatment deserved. In sadistic acts or relationships, the original dyadic relationship is repeated, only with the roles reversed. The child overtly identifies with the aggressor, but covertly relieves his or her own abuse through the suffering of the victim. These patterns can readily become ensconced as character traits. Children who have been abused often alternate between overt masochism and overt sadism, for in fact they are but opposite sides of the same internalized relationship. Why later in life boys tend toward sadistic character formation and girls toward overt masochism is, of course, an important and complex question, as is the treatment of these issues in adults. It nonetheless appears that the relational core is the same: the child internalizes and replicates *the dyadic relationship itself*. By re-creating the original abusive relationship, the child is able to maintain an abiding attachment to deeply needed others. This understanding can be particularly important in the treatment process, in helping the clinician recognize the presence of both sadistic and masochistic modes of relating to objects real or internal.

ON THE FUNCTION OF NEGATIVE INTROJECTS IN THE PSYCHE

The constant repetition of abusive relationships and an unshakable conviction of one's own badness are two of the most striking and pernicious problems of children who have been abused. Fairbairn (1952) expresses the same point when he speaks of the "obstinate attachment" that the abused have for their abusive internal objects (p. 117). Why does this occur? Why should an abused child continue to believe that he is absolutely bad, the cause of all his own suffering, and so wretched that he can only have human contact through abuse? Why should the child believe and act on these beliefs long after the abusive adult is no longer on the scene? Bowlby's (1988, pp. 108, 145) suggestion that children believe these things because they have been told that they are bad and punished misses the point rather seriously. Certainly children are blamed and degraded verbally by abusive adults. But in Bowlby's view, the *only* reason children think they are causally and morally responsible for bad treatment is that the abusive adults have told them that they are. This could hardly explain the absolute and unshakable conviction abused children have about these matters at the very core of the self, convictions strongly held well into adult life and despite the presence of new and better objects. Such basic assumptions about life and relationship must be held in place by strong psychological forces within the child and not simply by social reinforcement. The origin of this "obstinate attachment" is of such importance for understanding the therapeutic process with the abused and disturbed children that investigation of this issue is imperative. I believe this attachment to negative internal objects has several interrelated sources, which are discussed in the sections that follow.

Normal Developmental Egocentrism

The child's emotional and cognitive comprehension of the world, and of human relationships in particular, locates the child at the center of the events in his life. The exact nature of this normal and developmental pattern is, of course, a matter of ongoing study. But that some form of this "egocentrism" exists seems beyond dispute.

Defenses against Vulnerability

The sexually abused child typically experiences quite horrible states with little or no hope of controlling the external events and the resulting intrapsychic distress that ensues. To face such powerlessness, to know that the very people you most naturally want to rely on are unavailable or abusive, is to experience a loss of control and an extreme of vulnerability that is literally unthinkable. Feeling so powerless and vulnerable, the abused child adopts beliefs that have at least an illusory comfort, an illusion of control: "It is my badness that is making these things happen." This grandiosity allows the child the illusion that he could have prevented the original trauma and can prevent retraumatization by others. Hopkins (1984) speaks of how difficult it is for children to:

> give up idealized versions of their internal parents in order to recognize monstrous behavior in their actual parents. . . . This impasse can occur because the child prefers to feel responsible for, even guilty about, an external situation which he can control with the ambit of his omnipotence, rather than to admit his helplessness in the face of an intolerable reality. [pp. 69–70]

Identification with the Aggressor's View of the Self

One of the most orienting things for children is their parents' view of them. Children organize themselves around the conscious and unconscious actions, attitudes, beliefs, and affects that parents have about them. This begins early in life, with what is called social referencing, in the infant's and toddler's use of parental expressions and actions as fundamental clues to the nature of events in the child's experience and the range of actions and affects appropriate to these events. If the parent hates the child, the child will orient to and identify with this and thereby come to hate himself. The parent, because of forces and anxieties entirely internal to the parent, may project a negative identity onto the child. The child who is used in this psychological manner will assume that the role the parents have given him is correct and will come to see himself as hateful, worthless, perverse, and "bad." He will identify with the projection that has been foisted upon him. In extreme cases, such as Joey's, the child correctly perceives that the abuser wants to destroy him or indeed wants him dead (Rinsley 1980). The child correctly perceives this and assumes that the abuser's view of him is valid. This overt, destructive hostility toward the child is "soul murder" (Shengold 1989), and the child's identification with this view is a painful source of attachment to profoundly negative feelings about the self.

Nonrelatedness and the Attachment to Painful Introjects

It is clear from Fairbairn how the child takes on the burden of badness and idealizes the parent rather than face intolerable abuse alone. The weight and significance of this isolation is, I believe, deeper than terms like *aloneness* or *isolation* typically convey. As we shall see in the clinical material presented in Chapter 7, the child who tries to give up the only internal objects he has, namely abusive ones, faces annihilation anxiety. The child experiences a not unfounded fear of complete psychological disintegration. The terror and anguish of this state are, I believe, far beyond anything that most of us know as fear or aloneness. It is the experience of the self coming apart and beset by primitive terror. Faced with extreme, even psychotic, anxiety, the child feels in the depths of himself that it is better (or indeed necessary) to have a relationship to a bad object than to have no object to relate to. The child will elect to relate masochistically, sadistically, or perversely to both internal and real objects rather than face the unspeakable terror of nonrelatedness.

This struggle between unbearable emptiness and the relational conflicts contingent on the internalization of sadomasochistic models of relatedness is often expressed by disturbed children in frantic portrayal of what can accurately be called bulimic conflicts. For example, the child may create the story of a hungry shark who has not eaten "since the age of the dinosaurs," as Fred expressed it. The hungry shark will then eat something quite vulnerable, such as a baby, thereby expressing the child's sense that he has been devoured by the needs of others but also revealing the extent of his own object hunger. The devoured baby always turns out to be toxic, poisonous, or explosive—symbolizing the violence the child has had to internalize and his own resultant anger. The bomb will have to be vomited out if the shark is to live. But once the shark has vomited out this toxic introject, he is once again starving. These portrayals of bulimic relational dilemmas, with or without concurrent eating problems, are so frequent in the play of seriously disturbed children that one can become habituated to them and fail to appreciate how powerfully they express the problem of the child's longing for the abusive object: The child is starving, but the only object available for internalization is one that destroys the child from the inside.

When abusive and perverse relations are imposed upon emptiness and object hunger, the child is drawn into a basic dilemma of relatedness to bad objects: the child hungers for a person or relationship to internalize, but is forced to internalize what is toxic. The child starves in a world where all objects are poisonous.

Because early deprivation sets up such intense object longings, overt abuse that follows neglect can be more destructive of the child's psyche than abuse alone. The earlier emptiness forces the child to cleave to abusive relationships when they are offered. The capacity of object relations theory to articulate these pivotal dynamics rather than fall back on a concept such as "oral aggression," which really explains very little, is a strong reason for taking a relational rather than a drive view of the seriously disturbed or traumatized child.[3]

The attachment of abused children to pain and painful relationships appears to exist at a deeper psychic

---

3. While such intense orality is prevalent in the play of disturbed or traumatized children, the emphasis needs to be kept on the relational dynamics and not on the drive component. It would, I think, be a mistake to conclude that their orality or their aggression are endogenously stronger than that of other children or, more generally, that drives are at the core of human motivation. It is more plausible to believe that orality is so manifest because these children have had their relational needs thwarted from the beginning of life, when the oral expression of relational needs is paramount, and that so much aggression is present because they have been so much aggressed against and have responded to this with anger and identification with the aggressor.

level than one where well-defined representations of self and other interact in clear patterns ultimately accessible to memory. Children like Joey and Fred live chronically in states of irritation, agitation, or psychic malaise, as diffuse feelings of badness, anger, or shame come upon them. States of contentment or happiness are rare or nonexistent, something experientially foreign to them. One senses in such children an attachment to dysphoric affect, a kind of magnetic attraction toward painful states of the self and toward relationships that generate such feelings. The repetition of specific relational patterns likely serves to maintain the negative affective tone of painful early relationships.

Arthur Valenstein (1973) provides a most useful perspective on this adherence to negative affective states and relationships in his essay, "On Attachment to Painful Feelings and the Negative Therapeutic Reaction." He describes the nature and origin of those painful attachments made so early in life that all that now remains is "the aura of early experience" and fixation on "the primitive affect states characteristic" of "early trauma" (p. 375).

Valenstein suggests that painful relational states experienced early in life can, under certain conditions, come to constitute the bedrock experience of self and self in relation to others. In the first years of life, representations of self and other are not yet differentiated, and these painful states of relating are experienced by the infant or young child as constituting the nature not only of the other and of relationship but of the self as well. For children reared amid neglect and abuse, pain and painful relationship become part of the basic matrix out of which self and other are defined. Relatedness to some other person, Valenstein continues, is essential if the child is to develop even an imperfect sense of object constancy and internal stability. Pain becomes the proof that one exists and exists in relation to some other. Pain then expresses or symbolizes the psychological presence of the other. Finally, this painful sense of relating to the other becomes part of the self. If hurtful others and hurtful ways of relating are the only ones available, the infant will use these to develop an internalized sense of a "soothing" other. In this circumstance, the child would not simply think, "I *deserve* pain." Rather, the child feels, "I *am* this painful relationship," and ultimately, "I *am* this pain."

These deeply held affects are the bedrock of the person's psyche and "are emphatically held to because they represent the early self and self-object. Giving up such affects . . . would be equivalent to relinquishing a part of the self and/or self-object at the level which those affects represent" (Valenstein 1973, p. 376). We get a vivid sense of what this is in the clinical report that Valenstein gives. He describes a young male patient who struggled with considerable internal pain, loneliness, masochism, and depression. As a child he had been a head-banger and described his parenting in terms of Harlow's monkeys, which were raised in isolation by wire "mothers" who provided only food. The sensory hypersensitivity and somatized distress in which he lived re-created the pain one can readily imagine him experiencing as an infant and young child. Toward the end of his treatment he stated, "This discomfort in my body, roiling about all the time, cramping and pains—everything hurts and is uncomfortable; it is as if I hold on to it as the only thing I have ever known, the familiar, and I go back to it, uncomfortable though it is. It goes way back, as long as I can remember" (p. 388). He then adds, "I don't know how to do without it—this constant pain. Without it I would have nothing, and if I gave it up it would be like being different and like falling off a chair into space and being terrifyingly alone. It is as if I don't know how to be sensual in any other way and it does comfort me" (p. 388).

Valenstein does not give a full explication of what occurs when someone with such painful self-object representations attempts to give them up. The implied psychological consequences are severe, for the painful affects and thoughts are now a part of the self, the proof that one exists and exists in relation to some other person. The consequences are, I believe, made clear in Winnicott's (1962) notion of unthinkable anxieties. These are anxieties that date from the very formation of the self. Their occurrence signals not that something is happening *to* the self but that the self is coming apart. The potential for such anxieties is, in Winnicott's view, a central and defining characteristic of the human psyche. He states that "it is necessary not to think of the baby as a person who gets hungry, and whose instinctual drives may be met or frustrated, but to think of the baby as an immature being who is all the time *on the brink of unthinkable anxiety*" (p. 57). If the mother fails seriously in her empathic ministrations to the baby, the infant will experience this anxiety and will carry this experience, dread of it, and defenses against it through life. Unthinkable anxiety has, according to Winnicott, only a limited number of forms:

(1) Going to pieces
(2) Falling for ever
(3) Having no relationship to the body
(4) Having no orientation [p. 58]

We can see then that Valenstein's patient is even more deeply right than he knew. He fears that without his constant pain he would fall forever, alone, in a state of unthinkable anxiety.

This theory takes us to a most important point, to an understanding of why painful affect and negative selfobject representations are so deeply held: Without these painful introjects, the person is exposed to primordial states of psychological dissolution. There is nothing deeper, nothing good, in the psyche to hold onto. To give up experiences, no matter how painful, that convey a real sense of connection to others is to invite a terrifying and real sense of solipsistic isolation and psychic dissolution. Ultimately, then, *painful introjects are held to because of the fear of psychic annihilation.*

The power of this theory to explain masochistic dimensions of personality and the great difficulty people have in giving up attachments to negative objects cannot be underestimated. This attachment to pain explains the abused child's immense attraction to abusive relationships, feelings of complete badness, and resistance to change. Early masochistic attachments are so difficult to give up because pain and painful relationship constitute core aspects of the self, without which psychological identity, integrity, and relatedness all dissolve. The child will cleave to his sense of badness and to abusive templates of relationship as a way of preserving that internal pain that conveys the felt presence of the early object. For the child growing up amid pervasive neglect and abuse, the ties to the abusive parent and the bad internal object are paradoxically all the stronger because nothing good has been internalized. Without the tie to the bad object, the child is exposed to near autistic isolation and genuine disintegration of the psyche. Identification with the aggressor and sadomasochistic modes of relationship, in reality and fantasy, then become defenses against annihilation anxiety.[4]

---

4. It is important to point out in this context that a child need not experience overt abuse to be subject to extreme forms of emptiness and annihilation anxiety. Children who have been victims of pervasive early neglect or extreme psychological needs from the parent can also experience catastrophic disorganization and the evolution of tortured object relations. This is a point that Rinsley has tried to make in his own way.

The reverse argument can, however, also be made. It would appear to be the case that overt trauma can unravel the psyche of the older child or adult to primitive stages of emotional development that were ostensibly negotiated much earlier in life. Persons traumatized well past rapprochement can, it would seem, demonstrate the same relational dilemmas, primitive defenses, and annihilation anxiety as those victims of early neglect and later trauma that I have described (see Saunders and Arnold 1993). Of course, we could assume—perhaps too easily—that these older victims suffered covert neglect prior to traumatization. But we could also hypothesize that interpersonal trauma has the power to reach back into the past, as it were, and damage the psyche to its core. A third possibility, more akin to traditional views, would be that even more or less normal progress through the early stages of emotional development inevitably leaves a residue of primitive issues and conflicts that can be evoked by sufficient stress to the self later in life.

THEORETICAL SUMMARY

My fundamental suggestion, then, is that we understand
severely traumatized children as having internalized
object relations that are intolerable, inconsistent, unstable, and unlivable. The object relational dilemmas
have become ensconced as the basic working models
of self and other, of the possibilities of human relationship and life generally. The object relational dilemmas
I have described present the child with true dilemmas,
with unlivable patterns of relationship. Each is intrin-
sically unbearable: One cannot live thinking that one
has caused traumatic abuse to occur, nor can one live
thinking one is totally powerless to stop such abuse. The
child suffers not only the pain and anguish of each relational model but also the rapid transition from one
to the next. As we saw earlier, the child feels vulnerable
and afraid as a victim, and then shifts, psychologically
or in reality, into the position of abuser. But this role is
filled with terror and guilt, which drives the child to
self-punishment, and then the child feels again like a
victim. And so on. No role identity in the relational dilemmas provides any permanency, stability, or comfort.
Each belief, each role, is intolerable, and within the
entire pattern, there is no place of comfort or respite.

The traumatized child endlessly replicates these
unmetabolized introjects in play, in fantasy life, and in

The nature of the interconnections between the early stages of
emotional development, neglect, and later abuse are only imperfectly understood, to say the least. Understanding these connections
is, I believe, fundamental for the study of psychological trauma at
this time.

real relationships with peers and adults. He does this because he has no choice: for him, there are no other ways to be or to relate to others. The living out of these patterns is the repetition compulsion made manifest.

The relational dilemmas have their origin in the interconnected operation of the child's basic defensive responses to chronic abuse: identification with the aggressor, masochistic self-blame, and the seeking of object contact in sexualized or violent ways. The first two serve to protect the child from the complete vulnerability and abject powerlessness felt in traumatic events and relationships. Object contact is all the more desperately sought in the perverse ways abusing adults offer because the child feels so alone and so needy of relatedness. The three defensive processes generate the intrapsychic and interpersonal dilemmas that make psychic integration an impossibility.

These basic defensive operations are held in place by the fundamental need for connectedness and by the compelling threat of complete psychic disintegration. The psyche tolerates and indeed is forced to seek sado-masochistic modes of relatedness to prevent terrifying states of nonrelatedness and the upsurge of annihilation anxiety that this entails. This agonizing threat forces the child to adopt the extreme defenses we can so readily observe, and it makes the child resist giving up any part of the painful affects, beliefs, and modes of relationships that provide the only form of psychic stability he can imagine.

At this bleak juncture, it is worth pointing out that the overt manifestation of internalized relational models also serves certain positive purposes. As Blos (1971) has suggested, reliving and symbolic repetition are ways of concretizing, of making real and tangible that which has been awful, overwhelming, and conflictual. It is a way of stating a reality of experience that was never acknowledged or was actively denied by others. As part of the attempt to communicate incommunicable experiences and seek a new outcome, these repetitions do express a hope.

6

WHERE IS TRAUMA IN TRADITIONAL THEORY?

In the previous sections, I have described the internalized notions of self and other that the severely traumatized child typically develops. But what is the ultimate origin of these unmetabolized relational introjects, these basic representations of self and other? Naively, one might assume that they simply represent condensations from actual experiences or at least reflect actual experiences as understood and interpreted by the child. This perspective is implicit in the theoretical sources I have used—Ferenczi, Fairbairn, Berliner, and attachment theory. It is explicit, I believe, in much of the current research into early infant development and interpersonal interaction (e.g., Gianino and Tronick 1988, Stern 1985, Tronick and Gianino 1986). Traditional analytic theory does not, however, take this perspective and has a different view of early experience and its representation in the child's mind. The cluster of views that constitutes not only classical theory but also many of the modern theories of borderline conditions has tended to emphasize the endogenous and largely unconscious origins of the child's perceptions, feelings, and beliefs. The thesis that there are unconscious, developmental processes of mind that are relatively universal and only indirectly tied to actual experience is a fundamental part of Freud's contribution to modern thought. Even the theory I have presented, in which traumatic relationship plays such a significant role in shaping the child's internal life, puts considerable emphasis on relatively endogenous psychological processes, such as the child's fundamental need for human relatedness.

We shall see in this chapter, however, that while there may be a basic truth in the analytic notion of intrinsic processes of mind, there is a serious problem in the way the more traditional theories have so emphasized the internal and endogenous. The proper balance between individual history and universal psychic forces appears to have been lost in the push for innate causes of emotional distress. The standard theories of the origin of borderline conditions generally and the borderline child in particular have both participated in this trend. They are constructed with concepts that not only emphasize endogenous processes and deficits but also prevent the inclusion of traumatic interpersonal experience as a significant etiological factor. Revealing the theoretical and clinical consequences of this conceptual exclusion will, I hope, provide some genuine and nonpolemicized understanding of the difficulty that psychoanalytic thought has had in integrating a robust concept of interpersonal trauma.

In Chapter 5, we saw the usefulness of Kernberg's concept of unmetabolized, internalized object relations. But in the very same paper in which Kernberg (1966) proposed this concept, he shifts the etiological focus from real events and relationships to psychological processes said to be innate, universal, and constitutional. Kernberg's theory, for all its talk of object relations, does not ultimately attend to the reality of the child's interpersonal experience. Instead, we find a one-person psychology of constitutional predispositions and innate ego deficits that has nothing (or almost nothing) to do with actual relationships and their internalization. The events and processes that, in his view, ultimately cause borderline conditions are not relational ones but endogenous deficits in the capacity to master certain universal human conflicts and anxieties.

We can see all of this most clearly if we follow Kernberg's discussion of the child's integration of introjects, of basic representations of self and other. He suggests that through a process we do not fully understand, positive representations become consolidated and woven together into the general fabric of the self and into a basic sense of the possibilities of human relatedness. The negative representations of self and other, however, live on in relative isolation from one another, unintegrated into a coherent sense of self. Roughly speaking, the more disturbed the person, the more this is so. The negative representations of self and other exist not as memories or as structural foundations in the fabric of the self but as quasi-foreign intrusions that can at any moment take possession of the personality and generate the reenactment of relational templates.

It bears repeating what a powerful and useful descriptive theory this is. But Kernberg does *not* then discuss what we might expect—namely, those destructive early experiences that might contribute to the development of negative introjects. Instead of attending to the *content* of the object relational patterns observed in patients, the theory attends to the *structural* representation of these patterns in the mind, and their origin in innate, nonrelational processes of mind. There is no discussion of how early interpersonal experience might generate the intense affects, relational instability, or internal discontinuities that torment more disturbed people. Rather, Kernberg's theory maps out levels of psychic organization and different processes of internalization. In the more advanced processes, identification and ego-identity formation, there is considerable room for the impact of real persons, their actions and pathologies, on the psyche. But at the basic level, the introject level, actual experience of the other plays no role. At this level, the organizing (or disorganizing) forces come entirely from inside the nascent psyche.

We can see this clearly if we follow Kernberg's (1966) analysis of the origin of positive and negative introjects. The earliest organization of ego experience, he states, occurs through affects that express innate aggressive or libidinal drives. Experiences coalesce in the nascent ego around these affects and are kept separate "simply because they happen separately and because of the lack of capacity of the ego for integration" (p. 244). This generates a natural and non-pathological splitting that the ego uses to maintain order and reduce anxiety: the good and the bad, the aggressive and the libidinal are kept separate. In this way, all children have a reservoir of basic negative introjects simply because all those events that were internalized with aggressive affect fall into this category. The experiences are "bad" not because they reflect something bad that happened to the organism but because they were experienced in one drive–affect mode rather than the other.

Some children are able to metabolize these negative introjects into the larger and relatively cohesive structure of the self, and others are not. The focal question then becomes, Why are some children unable to metabolize their negative introjects? Why do some persons integrate the various positive and negative experiences of early life, whereas others keep these experiences so segregated, so split off from one another? Kernberg (1966) asserts that this failure of integration and the correlative reliance on defensive splitting results from "a pathological failure of ego development" in which "the *non*-object-relations [italics added] determined sub-structures of the ego are defective and interfere with the development of internalized object relations" (p. 250). This sort of nonrelational defect is, he claims, the cause of the more severe borderline and psychotic states. But even in the case of less pernicious splitting, the ultimate cause of the psyche's fragile and disordered state is an endogenous, nonpsychological defect, "a *constitutionally determined* [italics added] lack of anxiety tolerance interfering with the phase of synthesis of introjects of opposite valences" (p. 250). Kernherg briefly suggests that this problem with anxiety tolerance could be the result of too many negative introjects. But he then retreats from the implication that internalized real events interfere with psychological integration, for he quickly insists that the overabundance of negative introjects occurs because of the "*constitutionally determined* [italics added] intensity of aggressive drive derivatives and . . . severe early frustrations" (pp. 250–251). Kernberg again appears to create a small window for the role of actual experience when he states that early "frustrations" have some part in this. But what are these early frustrations? Here, Kernberg speaks entirely of drive and drive frustration. He does not speak of the relationship of parent and child in any broader sense. There is no theory of the impact of parental psychopathology on the child, no discussion neglect, abuse, or emotional exploitation. We find instead a traditional theory in which the parent is conceptualized only as failing to respond well enough to the child's libidinal or aggressive drives. This poorness of fit is implicitly seen as accidental or as largely the result of the innate overabundance of drive energy in the child. The consequences of relational failure are conceptualized entirely in terms of a one-person psychology, not really in terms of relationship at all.[1]

---

1. I think it is fair to say, as Greenberg and Mitchell (1983, p. 336 ff.) point out, that Kernberg's theory has evolved since its initial presentation. In later works (Kernberg 1976), the organizing impact of object relational experience comes more to the fore, and the role of innate drives or affects recedes. The shift in emphasis in metapsychology does not, however, appear to have led Kernberg to a greater understanding of the role of parental pathology, overt trauma, or relational dynamics. The metapsychology may have changed, but there is no theory of traumatic early object relations to back this up. For this reason, I find that Kernberg's later views are not appreciably more useful than the earlier ones. My

We see a similar picture if we look at Fred Pine's (1986) paper "On the Development of the 'Borderline-Child-to-Be.'" Pine offers a "model" (p. 451), a generalized theory of the epigenesis of borderline disorders of childhood. He suggests that borderline pathology in children requires "the experience of early trauma, the evolution of developmental deficits, and the construction of survival mechanisms . . . which are adhered to desperately and become pathological defenses" (p. 451). This model is surely correct in the broad sense that Pine intends.

The relevant question, however, is what constitutes "early trauma"? Pine (1986) gives a clear answer, one that conceptualizes trauma entirely in terms of innate intensity of drives and equally innate deficits in basic ego capacities. He asserts that trauma is the result of "high inborn or early-forming aggressivity or libidinal pressure, deficits in the ordinarily inborn ability to sort experience, intrusive or destructive parental inputs, and those adventitious circumstances in development such as severe pain and early illness" (p. 453). While apparently wanting to give some role to parental behavior, Pine speaks very little of this. Overt abuse and neglect are not mentioned. Much of the article deals with illness, physical pain, and their psychological conse-

---

point is not to single out Kernberg's theories for criticism but to make a general and more important point, namely that a clinically useful relational theory cannot be created simply by altering the metapsychology of pre-existing views. The observation and formulation of specific dynamics, and an understanding of the implications for the treatment process, are necessary in the development of theories that make substantial additions to our knowledge.

quences, and not with the pathogenic effects of parental behavior, intentions, or personality deficits. Pine further diminishes the significance of interpersonal factors by repeatedly referring to "the traumatic stimulus." Terms of this nature emphasize events and physical processes and take our attention away from the character of relationships and processes within them.

The one interpersonal factor Pine does discuss directly is what he calls the "mis-match" between the young child's needs and the mother's ministrations. His conceptualization of how this affects the child is noticeably less elaborate and less relational than Rinsley's (1978, 1980, 1985), which was discussed in Chapter 3. Pine (1986) asserts that this interactional mismatch simply creates "too much noise in the psychic system" (p. 452). When the child's ego functions are not given the support they need, they are overwhelmed by "inborn" drives or disruptive physical events. In Pine's theory, this overloading of the ego functions, this psychic meltdown, *is* trauma. The actual nature of the mismatch with the mother or father plays no causal role. Dysfunctions in the parent–child relationship leave the ego weak and vulnerable, but the character of the relationship is not a factor. In this theory, the failures or assaults of adults are, in the initial stages of life, not even perceived or represented in the child's mind. Understandably, there is no notion in Pine's theory that disruptions in the parent–child relationship could affect the child's conception of self and other, and there is no mention of the relational dynamics so apparent in traumatized children like Joey and Fred.

In addition, Pine's (1986) theory discounts the child's capacity to represent events and relationships accurately and emphasizes the child's capacity to over-interpret or misinterpret events that have engendered ego disruption: "It is the child's experience of the stimulus which must be emphasized; the stimulus itself may not be externally identifiable as traumatic. [Further,] it is not the objective behavior of the other, but rather, how that behavior is experienced by the child that is laid down in memory and carried" (p. 452). There is surely a sense in which these claims are true. It is virtually tautological that it is the experience of relationship that is represented and remembered. But Pine's theory has already excluded any full or articulated experience of relationship from the child's representational abilities. The end result is a theory in which the child is implicitly understood as developing distorted, unrealistic interpretations of relationship because minor, earlier failures of nurturance led to psychic disruption.

We can see, then, that Pine's concept of trauma is problematic in two interrelated respects: the range of potentially traumatic events is quite limited, and the theory used to portray and explain the nature of trauma prevents the inclusion of relational pathology. The events considered traumatic are largely impersonal impingements on the functioning of the ego apparatus at an early age. The theory levels out any special or unique effects of interpersonal or interactional pathology, including sexual abuse. External traumata become nonspecific, in that they are all reduced to their generic effects on ego processes. The *nature* of the traumatic event is largely unimportant because it is not, at least early on, represented or remembered by the child. The child is basically only aware of the "noise" that events create in the psyche, not the events themselves. If the theory were true, the psychic imprint of the parents' actions or personalities on the child would be a very limited one indeed. The effects of real relationships upon the child's conception of self and others are simply not a part of this theoretical vocabulary. In such a conceptual framework, interpersonal trauma cannot make an appearance.

In Pine's ego-psychological theory, as in many traditional views, the infant is seen as being incapable of having elaborated representations of self and other. This view in turn seems to be derived from the view that the young infant is trapped within an autistic phase, to use Mahler's term (Mahler et al. 1975), and only slowly and imperfectly comes to an awareness of the existence and nature of others. Part of the reason Kernberg, Pine, and others may be so drawn to innate factors in the origin of severe pathology is that this notion of an autistic phase precludes the idea that the young child could represent the images of self and other necessary for a relational view of trauma. The original form of these theories of infantile solipsism in psychodynamic theory is Freud's (1940) notion of primary narcissism. In this light, one can appreciate even more fully the powerful critique of this concept by Michael Balint in *The Basic Fault* (1969).

Overall, we see that Kernberg (1966) and Pine (1986) both assert that the fundamental sources of borderline pathology are largely in constitutional factors, either overendowment of drives or deficits in the ego capacities that sort and organize experience. They are surely correct that innate deficits of ego-integrative capacities (however this concept might be spelled out) and early physical trauma can seriously affect a child's psychological development. I suspect that most people who work with borderline or traumatized children believe that these factors often play an important etiological role. Emphasis on these factors, however, turns our attention away from other factors that may shape the child's personality and development, such as overt trauma. The more closely these two theories are examined, the more one sees how thoroughly real events and relationships are not only excluded from causal roles but also left unconceptualized. The conceptualization of early experience in both theories tends to minimize the impact other people and relational events can have. In Kernberg's theory, the role that could be played by actual relationships and their impact on the child is replaced by constitutionally determined deficits in the capacity to integrate disparate experiences. Pine presents us with a theory in which early object relations cannot get a foothold and in which the pivotal early disruptions are understood as the result of drive intensity and deficits in ego functions.

We can now see in somewhat broader terms why analytic perspectives on seriously disturbed children have had difficulty incorporating and understanding interpersonal trauma. As has often been correctly noted, Freudian theory and its variants are all theories of trauma: the oedipal crisis, separation-individuation, and failures of selfobject availability all present the psyche with inevitable yet overwhelming disruption that requires significant reorganization of the psyche to a "higher" level but also to a level where neurotic compromise is virtually inevitable. Children who have been abused would appear to have to deal with overt trauma and the special psychic burdens it imposes in addition to these normative, developmental crises. Kernberg's and Pine's theories not only fail to articulate this point but develop a conceptual framework that necessarily tends to absorb overt trauma into developmental trauma.

If, as Kernberg and Pine imply, disturbed and healthy children differ only in their innate integrative capacities, and if psychic development consists of mastering universal forms of intrapsychic conflict, we can infer that at a sufficiently high level of abstraction, all children have the same emotional history. All children suffer drive frustration; all children go through universal and difficult experiences of individuation, isolation, and powerlessness; all children must integrate positive and negative, libidinal and aggressive experiences. What appears to be unique and injurious in personal experience (such as traumatic relationship) is replaced by this universal developmental history and the nonrelational failures of innate ego capacities. The differences between the normal child and the disturbed, abused child are based not on the differences in experience but on the different abilities to master what is universal and inevitable in human experience. These traditional theories blur an important distinction between normative developmental trauma and overt trauma that has no developmental necessity whatsoever. It would appear that this distinction will have to be reinstituted and careful attention given to the role of actual experience if traditional psychodynamic theory is to integrate the concept of overt trauma in a genuine way.

This fundamental conceptual flaw unfortunately vitiates Kernberg's gripping and useful theoretical metaphor—that the disturbed child or adult suffers from unmetabolized introjects. If disturbed children have unmetabolized introjects, normal children must have metabolized introjects. If disturbed and normal children differ only in their metabolic capacities, one can again infer that all children have essentially the same introjects, good and bad alike, regardless of overt trauma. We are thus again at universal developmental history, and the role of actual experience cannot find a foothold.

The same conviction in universal history appears if we examine the notion of regression as used in Kernberg (1966) and in classical analytic theories. When adults regress, either in the containing context of the psychotherapeutic relationship or injuriously in the context of their lives, what do we see? Is it some reflection of their unique personal history, or is it the revelation of a universal human past? Is the splitting observed in adult borderlines part of universal human experience that the rest of us have surmounted, or is it a continued manifestation of a common but by no means universal form of early relational trauma? One's answers to these questions have considerable consequences, both for clinical practice and for theory itself. One of the most powerful philosophical and clinical notions in all of Freudian theory is the idea that both regression and pathology point us to human nature itself, that in pathology and regression we can find the universal structures, needs, and conflicts of human life. Once this view is given up, the empirical scope and the philosophical grandeur of the theory are transformed. If the pathology of children like Joey and Fred does not simply reveal universal early stages of emotional development, we are operating on new ground. Psychological development would have to be reconceptualized to account for actual experience; emotional pathology would point to concrete and personal history as well as to normative stages poorly negotiated or defects in innate endowment. The tie between emotional illness and regression begins to loosen in an analogous way: the normative stages of early emotional development, the regressed state of the traumatized child, and the regression observed in the healthier child or adult are seen to be three distinct processes and not simply one process seen from different points of view. The true integration of trauma into dynamic theory requires reexamination and reformulation of powerful views that inspired and energized classical theory.

Kernberg's theory, reflective of classical theory generally, has then three interrelated theses: that we all have essentially the same emotional past and, thus, the same introjects; that what differentiates the disturbed child from the normal child is the failure of nonrelational, constitutional, integrative capacities; and that regression and pathology both reveal the universal human past. It is, I believe, the common assumption of these three views that explains why an integration of the concept of interpersonal trauma into traditional analytic theory has not yet taken place.

Contrary to Kernberg's and Pine's theories of constitutional deficits, it would appear to be more consistent with the clinical data and more useful theoretically to think of traumatized children as having internalized the neglectful, sexual, or violent relationships to which they have been exposed. This process then requires the child to take extreme defensive maneuvers to cope with the unresolvable dilemmas of relationship and the underlying threat of nonrelatedness. The introjects of traumatized children are, in this view, simply different and "worse" than those of children who have not suffered such violations. These introjects are harder to metabolize, not because of innate aggression or failures of integrative capacity but because the introjects encode horrific experience, impossible conflicts, and extreme defenses. The child cannot live, for example, thinking that he is completely vulnerable, but he cannot live thinking that he is utterly bad and the cause of his own violation. These dilemmas, and the anxiety they entail, literally tear the psyche apart and expose the child to the threat of psychic annihilation. It is this, and not innate deficits or innate aggression, that creates the torment and disorder we see in traumatized children.

The theory of relational dilemmas I propose, in which the introjects of the abused are worse than those of us who have had more benign childhoods, does not eliminate endogenous processes of mind. Far from it. The relational dilemmas that develop in the psyche of the abused child are based in core human needs for security, care, and relatedness. When these basic needs are unmet, the child is threatened with psychic annihilation, and must take extreme defensive maneuvers to preserve a sense of self, and a sense of self in relation to others. This can all too easily lead to identification with the aggressor, self-blame, and the finding of relatedness perversely. The basic needs, however defined, are surely innate. The compensatory defensive operations are virtually inevitable in the face of serious neglect and abuse. While not universal in the sense of being developmentally programmed and independent of experience, they are causally inevitable under certain conditions. Deprive the organism of basic interpersonal connectedness and expose it to abuse, and they appear. They appear so early and so strongly because the need of the child for care and attention is so great and their absence so overwhelming. The full-blown manifestation of identification with the aggressor, self-blame, perverse object seeking, and annihilation anxiety require, if I am correct, the impact of real events and relationships on the underlying psychological needs of the child. By attending to the interplay of traumatic relationship and basic needs and anxieties, the theory I have presented tries to find a better balance of the historic and the innate in the development of emotional distress and psychic disorder.

7

THE DILEMMA OF THERAPY AND THE USES OF VIOLENCE

> The release of bad objects from the unconscious is one of
> the chief aims which the psychotherapist should set him-
> self out to achieve, even at the expense of a severe "trans-
> ference neurosis"; for it is only when the internalized bad
> objects are released from the unconscious that there is any
> hope of their cathexis being dissolved.
>
> — W. R. D. Fairbairn

For the sexually traumatized child, the very idea of therapy is fraught with anxiety. Such a child comes to therapy with intense and genuine needs: suffering from great distress, fragmentation, and primitive conflict, he wishes to convey his inner torment and desperately hopes the therapist can heal him. The abused child wants to convey disorganized, frightening, and repulsive feelings, all the while believing that if he does convey them, it will cost him the very relationship that he wants and needs so much. The child fears that the therapist will abandon or abuse him because his feelings are perverse, violent, or bizarre; that he can *get* the therapist to abandon or abuse him; and that he could injure or abuse the therapist. Entering into a relationship with the therapist means risking not only retraumatization but causing this abuse or abandonment. In overt or covert ways, the child will test these fears and convictions. The conflict between intense longings for relatedness and fear of what will happen in relationship can easily lead to anxiety, confusion, emotional withdrawal, and highly distorted forms of communication.

The conflict between longing for relationship and fear of traumatic repetition in relationship make transference issues pivotal in the psychotherapeutic treatment of traumatized children. To see, by way of example, how this is so let us return to Fred and his revelation of sexual abuse in drawings and stories, described in Chapter 2. Just before this central revelation, Fred sang a little song that went like this: "Dr. Prior's found the love he's been looking for. . . . He's going to hump and fuck and sweat through the night. . . . He's going to fuck me, hump me. . . ." I forcefully said four times in a row, "How scary it would be if you thought I was really going to do that." It was then, and only then, that Fred made the "hidden videotape" of the abuse he had suffered and made the drawings that conveyed the horror of his abuse. It was only after this transferential fear was addressed that Fred was able to reveal what had actually occurred to him.

In the initial stages of treatment, the child's immense pain and longing for relationship can lead to a frantic and chaotic rush to convey his torment, despite the deeply felt risks. Boys like Joey and Fred often want to use therapy for the expression of violent, sadomasochistic feelings. This violent play is the child's way of bringing his issues and fears to treatment, of making real contact with the therapist, and of making the unintegratable experiences he has lived through tangible for the therapist and himself. These experiences and the solutions attempted so far are delivered to the therapist for understanding and comfort and in the hope that the therapist can heal and integrate all that has happened to the child. The presence of such violent play is thus a sign of the therapeutic alliance.

This violent play, and the fear of its effect on the therapist, can, however, be quite disorganizing for the child, who has likely struggled for a considerable time to control his impulses. It can also be quite confusing and frightening for the therapist, who may in fact have countertransferential feelings of horror and disgust, just as the child imagines. It can be difficult for the therapist, the family, and the treatment system to see the value of chaotic, destructive play in a child who is already violent and fragmented and who may be made even more anxious by the permission to express his thoughts and feelings. The therapist may fear that he or she is allowing the child to be retraumatized by undigested memories and affects, precipitating an uncontained regression, or encouraging the child to be violent toward others. The therapist may naturally feel inclined to suppress the child's violent or disorganized play. There surely are times when the regulation of affect, the containment of behavior, and the enhancement of ego strengths are absolutely essential in the treatment of sexually traumatized children. In a sense, such disturbed children need these all the time.

If the therapist fails, however, to respond openly enough to these violent overtures by the child, the treatment may never truly begin. If the therapist rejects the primitive, sadomasochistic play, he or she may well *confirm* in the child's mind that the core of the child's self *is* bad, that adults cannot understand or tolerate who he is or what he has experienced, and that if the child conveys who he is, he will be rejected. The therapist who fears retraumatizing the child with exposure to violent memories and impulses may actually run the risk of retraumatizing the child by rejecting the only way the child knows to convey the reality of his experience. All too often, this rejection by the therapist replicates the chronic pattern of the child's life in the family, schools, or treatment system—of being rejected by adults and institutions for aggressive or perverse behavior that he cannot control and that expresses the realities of his life and his feelings. Rejected and blamed by caring adults, the child feels once again that he is bad and that he causes bad things to happen in relationships, even with the best of people. This generates intense guilt and despair that the child suffers completely alone.

Fearing abandonment for his violent impulses and memories, the child may attempt to maintain a relationship with the good therapist by killing off the "bad self." As Ekstein (1966) describes in his essay "The Working Alliance with the Monster," the child says, in effect, to the therapist, " Let's love each other but hate my monster" (p. 406). As we saw earlier with Joey and Fred, the child hopes the therapist will ally with his good side and that together they will destroy the bad that is in him. But the bad self is, for better or worse, very much a part of who the child is. It encodes what he has experienced and internalized in life and contains his frantic search for safety. If the child and therapist succeed in walling off the bad self, the therapy proceeds in an illusion of completeness. What is created is a problematic form of the corrective emotional experience, in which only the

Good Self is therapized. The split-off Bad Self is not metabolized. It goes further underground, demands immense amounts of psychic energy for its control, constantly threatens to take possession of the child's whole psyche, and gains control of the child's overt behavior during times of anxiety, loss, or developmental transition. These patterns can continue in adult life and may explain how the allegedly therapized child becomes an abuser later in life. Successful treatment requires integration of the Bad Self and the experiences, impulses and relational patterns encoded in this identity, no matter how difficult this may be.

When the therapist engages in safe and contained ways with the child's violence, a number of positive results occur. First, the child is able to share his experience with a sympathetic and comforting person. The therapist has ample opportunity to express how unfair, unjust, and damaging the experiences were and how wrong it was of the perpetrator to hurt the child. Second, the therapist can articulate the many aspects of the experience that the child may have recorded but could not organize into coherent thoughts or feelings, either because the trauma was so overwhelming or because the child's cognitive and emotional development was incomplete. Labeling feelings and giving descriptions of events can give such children the beginnings of a verbal means of expressing and managing their memories. Third, as the therapy progresses, the therapist can begin to articulate with the child the vulnerability of being abused, the wish to identify with the aggressor as a way of preventing vulnerability and renewed abuse, and guilt over being aggressive like the perpetrator. The manifestation of these patterns in the child's current life can be interpreted in light of these underlying patterns. And fourth, the therapist can help the child find his underlying relational needs, the longings for love, care, and affection that lie beneath his aggressive and sexualized modes of obtaining object contact.

This work requires much more of the therapist than simply allowing or containing violent play. The therapist must become engaged as an active and interpretive force in the play. To attempt to be neutral or in some way a "blank screen" would amount to abandoning the child to reexperience disintegrating feelings and memories alone. Enduring the suffering alone, with no one to go to for protection, comfort, or understanding, is surely part of what made the abusive events traumatic in the first place. When, however, the therapist enters the violent play, a variety of clinical difficulties ensue. Violent play that allows for the therapeutic working through of traumatic experiences often requires walking a fine line between repetition that is itself traumatic and repetition that allows for mastery and the discovery of new modes of object relating. Finding this line may be a *creation* by the child and the therapist and not the discovery of anything clearly demarcated in the child's psyche. How, in practice, to get close enough to the trauma without stepping over into traumatic reenactment requires considerable tolerance for anxiety by child and therapist alike. Struggling together to demarcate dangerous overstimulation and productive working through can enhance the child's damaged ego capacities to notice, organize, and regulate affective states. The therapist, using his or her own empathic capacity, monitors the boundary between play and retraumatization, between expression and possession. The therapist can shift or modulate the action and affect and convey the comforting sense that he or she will regulate the boundary between memory and reenactment. As this process is repeated, the child begins to develop an internalized sense of these affective boundaries and to use his own defenses to prevent emotionally injurious events from occurring. The capacity for the safe and useful expression of traumatic memories and affects is thereby created.

As the treatment progresses, the child will likely express the relational fears and dilemmas in play or in the relationship with the therapist. The seriously disturbed child will, however, often resist interpretation of these dilemmas, no matter how clear the material may be and no matter how the therapist may try to convey interpretive ideas. The child's overall fragmentation and the fears of rejection or retraumatization can be strong enough to prevent effective work on these central concerns. Fears about the treatment relationship and affective memory of traumatic events may both be subjected to primitive and powerful defenses. Basic concerns and memories may he isolated and walled off in the child's psyche or dispersed in a generalized fragmentation. At the extreme, this amounts to what Bion (1959) called "attacks on linking," the psyche's primitive defensive attempt to protect against pain by destroying all meaning and interconnectedness of thought, feeling, and action. The child resists interpretation of the transference because agonizing fears and memories are thereby dredged to the surface and because interpretation implicitly asks the child to give up deeply held attachments to abusive objects. It is common with traumatized children to see not only resistance to the clarification or interpretation of basic relational dilemmas and transference fears but negative therapeutic reactions as well. The child responds to correct and appropriate interpretations with ever stronger clinging to old and painful feelings and relationships.

When the therapist meets such intense resistance to interpretations that seem manifest in the child's play, he or she may pull back, for fear of intrusively stating what the child cannot bear to hear, indoctrinating the child, or interfering with the therapeutic alliance. Certainly there can be a danger of forcing interpretations on the child that are simply inaccurate, or moving forward before the issues are sufficiently organized in the child's mind, or delving into difficult issues before the child feels safe enough in the relationship. But the risk on the other side is of colluding with the child's primitive resistances. If the therapist fails to articulate the relational dilemmas that animate the child's life, the child will likely be too disorganized, anxious, and alone to do so. Some amount of integrative energy must come from the therapist. Active articulation and explanation of the relational dilemmas in a manner accessible to the child are, in my experience, generally necessary with severely traumatized and disturbed children.

For most therapists, the point in this work that is most difficult is when the child asks the therapist to abuse him. For the seriously abused child, human relationship presents, as we have seen, only two ultimate possibilities: be an abuser or be abused. The therapist will often find him- or herself assigned to either the victim role or the perpetrator role, with only tenuous permission to be an observer or ally. Most therapists are quite comfortable playing the victim role or speaking for the child in that role. To be the perpetrator, to engage in play or drama in which the child is attacked, hurt, or violated by the therapist's role persona, is often another matter. It is easy to see why. As such play becomes more robust, displacement is lost by both therapist and child, and the play begins to resemble the very events that traumatized the child in the first place. Few therapists are so comfortable with their aggression that they can easily move into the role of a sadistic sexual abuser, even if the child invites this sort of play. Play with the therapist in the aggressive role provides, however, important avenues for therapeutic progress. Most obviously, play in which the child is once again the victim re-creates the original traumatizing events and relational patterns. The child can then come very close to reexperiencing the abuse he suffered, with all the contingent feelings and defensive operations, including identification with the aggressor, the need to find relatedness perversely, and the conviction that he caused the abuse to occur. All these dynamics are then open for interpretation.

Why getting dangerously close to reenactment can be so transformative of core dynamics is one of the more important questions about the therapeutic process. That it is transformative, at least for some patients, seems undeniable. Two reasons that it may be mutative for traumatized children have already been mentioned. First, reenactment is necessary if the child is to feel truly heard and joined by the therapist. The benign and helpful other is irrelevant in the child's basic relational templates. If the child can experience relationship only in the paradigm of abuser-abused, and if the transference perception of the therapist as abuser is intensely held by the child, some degree of reenactment is necessary simply to allow for sufficiently deep and real communication of these fundamental beliefs and feelings. Second, it is through partial reenactment that the events, relationships, feelings, and defenses that constitute the original traumatic relationship can be most directly addressed in the therapy. It is my hypothesis that a third (and as yet barely explored) aspect to this issue involves the abused child's problems with the internalization of good objects and relationships. If the child thinks of himself as inherently bad and deserving of abuse, he will be unable to internalize the kindness and caring of others, including the therapist. Rejection and abuse will feel real and confirm the child's sense of who and what he is. Positive experiences will be unable to penetrate the barrier of fixed beliefs of badness and will not adhere to the child's core sense of self. What may initially be experienced is only that the therapist is less abusive than the original objects, is a different sort of abuser. The child assumes the therapist is a wolf in sheep's clothing, someone who acts nice but who is, underneath the facade, just as bad as the other people he has known. As the child's anxieties about relationship and defenses are worked through, and as the outlines of real memory of trauma begin to emerge, the child can come to see that the therapist is a sheep in the wolf's clothing of his transferential perceptions. Using another metaphor, we could say that the therapist must be a reverse Trojan horse—bad enough to be taken in, but then working to good effect once internalized. As the difference between past and present, abusive objects and therapist is slowly recognized, more and more of the benign nature of the therapist can be internalized. The child's negative sense of himself begins to change, and the dilemmas consequent to abuse begin to lose their grip on the child's psyche. The metabolization of the toxic, transferential image of the therapist is essential for the internalization of a new sense of self and others. The case report that follows will clarify some of these complex and important points.

8

A CASE STUDY

Our suggestion is that in therapeutic work we must start with the acceptance of the delusional monster and bring about a working alliance with that part of the patient's personality. At a later point of the process we will have helped the patient to accept and to synthesize the monster parts of himself as well as the patient's feelings about the therapist. The interpretive strategy of the taming of the monster, analogous to Freud's dictum that where id was shall ego be, suggests that where unstable introjects ruled, capacity for object relations shall be developed.

—RUDOLF EKSTEIN

The metabolization of the unstable introjects of an abused child is a complex and difficult therapeutic endeavor. The rigid, contradictory relational patterns that are so strongly internalized must be brought to the surface, contained, interpreted, reworked in the relationship with the therapist and finally synthesized into a new sense of self and other. To convey the ways in which the core relational dilemmas are manifested in a psychotherapeutic treatment, the manner in which primitive anxieties hold these dilemmas in place, and the pivotal role of the transference relationship, I shall review here a three-and-a-half-year therapy, consisting of 411 sessions, with a boy named Damon.

Damon came to the hospital at the age of 8 because he was violent and unmanageable. He had attacked several women; in the last incident, he went after a baby-sitter with some large scissors. At the hospital, he was initially withdrawn, frightened, and disorganized. He could barely attend to any person or activity. Instead, he appeared to respond to internal stimuli and would act accordingly. Walking down a hallway, he could be seen dodging and deflecting imaginary explosions. Damon had immense difficulty forming relationships with peers and staff. Held in any form of physical restraint, he would become panic-stricken, scream, and regress. He would occasionally "go wild": his eyes would glaze over, and he would attack anyone around him.

Damon was even more fully fragmented than Joey or Fred. Though outwardly inhibited much of the time, his play revealed primitive and violent fantasies. Early in the treatment, he used dolls to play out a sexual assault on a woman. In this story it was very unclear whether he was one of the abusers or a "needle man" (like the physicians at the hospital) who might help the young woman. Suddenly, he bent the arms and legs of the female doll backward, and she became a giant spider who ate up those who were abusing her and then the whole world, with her genitals.

Damon had not been subject to a pattern of torture like Joey's. But since infancy he had witnessed the physical abuse of his mother and was chronically exposed to adult sexuality. Damon's father was described by those who knew him as a distant and lonely man, suspicious, and quite possibly paranoid. He had teased Damon with some degree of sadism, though he had at times given nice gifts to Damon and his younger sister. When the parents separated (when Damon was 6), Damon and his sister had visits with the father. During

these visits, the father began to abuse the little girl sexually, with increasing levels of physical intrusion and
assault. When he finally engaged in intercourse with his
daughter, with Damon watching, her screams brought
the police, who knocked down the door and arrested
him on the spot. Damon fought with them to protect
his father. The father was never brought to trial, for reasons that were never explained. Damon's mother was
an insecure and vulnerable woman who had been able
to distance herself psychologically from her quite
troubled past. She had been able to put her life together
in a more responsible way but was initially rather distant and uninvolved with Damon's treatment. She had
a certain underlying sweetness and a genuine wish for
Damon's recovery. She eventually began to participate, did some therapeutic work of her own with me,
and expressed the hope of becoming a counselor for
troubled children.

This then, was the overt and accepted history,
though Damon denied any knowledge of it. Those involved in Damon's treatment came to suspect, however,
that something else must have occurred. His great fear
of men, his overt anxieties about anal penetration and
oral ingestion, and his graphic play of fellatio and anal
intercourse naturally led us to suspect that he had been
sexually abused by his father. Conclusive proof never
appeared in the course of treatment. Even at the very
end of our therapy work, when Damon played out
graphic scenes of witnessing the sexual assault of a girl,
he did not portray himself being abused in any fashion.

Initially, Damon came to therapy twice a week. Our
first meetings were spent mixing colored water and inks
at the sink and engaging in horribly violent and sexual

play with doll figures. In these violent and sexual stories there was a complete lack of safety, restraint, or relief from the onslaught. A central event in the first months of treatment was my introduction of the "Safe Place." This small plate with three tiny animals on it was the only place in the universe safe from sex and violence. To maintain its safety, I eventually had to physically restrain Damon from destroying it. My willingness and ability to protect the Safe Place meant a great deal to him.

Damon's doll play often contained the bulimic dilemmas described in Chapter 5. Typically, a huge and hungry shark would eat babies. This represented what had happened to Damon, to his childhood, but also his object hunger. The eaten baby would invariably turn out to be a poison bomb that would have to be vomited out if the shark was to live. This element expressed Damon's understandable fear of internalizing bad objects. Once the shark vomited up the baby, he would be starving again, and the cycle would repeat indefinitely. The dilemmas contingent on starving in a sea of bad objects could not be more stark. It should come as no surprise that Damon was quite anxious about eating, especially foods that contained fluids, like milk on cereal.

In both the doll play and the water play, I was struck by Damon's complete disorganization and his inability to relate to me in any overt way. Indeed, he virtually ignored me in most of our sessions. While "doing colors," he would mix his colors and pour them down the sink. I would watch, offering observations and comments—all of which were ignored. If I tried to enter the play with characters of my own, I was ignored. There was a glimmer of connection between us at the beginning of sessions and at the end, but within them I began to feel disconnected, lost, hopeless, and bored.

Ekstein (1966) describes this mode of relating to others in borderline psychotic children as "autistic." He does not mean, of course, that a child like Damon would be diagnosed as autistic. His point is that some borderline children are so overtly disconnected that those working with them clinically are reminded of autistic remoteness. The borderline child in this state unconsciously but intentionally severs all outward signs of communication and relatedness as a defense against transference fears. The expression and working through of these fears becomes an essential part of the treatment, as we shall see. Ekstein describes the next two general phases of the therapeutic relationship as "symbiotic" and "neurotic" and suggests that there is a slow evolution from the autistic through the symbiotic to the neurotic. He states, however, that this shift is by no means irreversible (p. 104). This general pattern did, in fact, occur in my work with Damon. How these fundamental shifts in relationship come about is part of the story of this chapter.

The transference anxieties described in Chapter 7 appeared in various ways. In Damon's play, I began to observe a combination of primitive longings for a good father, identification with the aggressor, fears of my abusing him, and fears of being poisoned. Dilemmas about closeness to me were tangibly demonstrated as early as our fifteenth session, in which we were briefly able to talk about a real event. At school, a boy had accidentally hit Damon on the head with a ball. As we discussed the incident and Damon slowly grasped something of the distinction between accidental and intentional injuries, he told me that once his father had intentionally pulled the inner tube out from under him at a lake and he had sunk, not knowing how to swim. I said that must have been scary. He then said we would need to meet for 100 weeks. But as we examined a "blown-up" car, he said it would have to be 200 weeks. (In fact, it·turned out to be 186.) I said, "So you like coming here to my office to fix things." He said, "Yes," but then he suddenly grabbed an undeniably phallic baby's bottle filled with a milky fluid and sucked it with energy and abandon. Aware of the obvious double meaning of sucking such a bottle and sensing his anxiety, I asked if he really wanted to do that. He said, "No, but I have to, to get strong." In our next session, everyone was killed by "Skeletor," leader of the evil forces. As Skeletor, I made up fluids that could chase Damon around the room. When I stated how scary it would be if I really turned into Skeletor, Damon played out a story of oral sex between a man and a boy. In the sessions that followed, we would often spend some time trying to divide "the good oxygen" from "the bad oxygen"— "so they don't mix." The problem was that the good oxygen always had to have some bad in it, "for strength." But once included, it would pollute the good. If someone breathed this polluted oxygen, he would die or turn bad and require punishment. Thus, the good would leave him weak, but the bad would destroy him from within.

Here we see how the child's underlying relational needs and traumatic early relationships generate relational dilemmas. Damon longed to incorporate me, because of his profound inner emptiness and his hunger for a father who would love him and fix him. This wish to internalize a good male object was experienced as a condensation of oral needs and invasive adult sexuality: sucking on a penis that gives milk. Even though he recognized that the milk and the sucking were dangerous, he had to proceed, for he would be weak unless he took in this fluid that was partially bad and aggressive. The relational wish for a good object was transformed into a perverse wish/fear of sexual contact that replicated a terrifying trauma but that also repeated a powerful and "nurturing" mode of object contact that held the promise of making him strong. The dilemma could not be more bleak: he can have a relationship, but only at the cost of abuse that is poisonous. Without the relationship, he will starve or be weak. Starving, he tries to take in an object in the only manner that he knows. But then he has brought about his own abuse and the consequent poisoning. Splitting what is internalized into good and bad components and splitting the self in the same way will not work, so there is no way out. (Incidentally, we see here why many abused children cannot *attain* splitting. We also see how much more detailed an account object relations theory can give of these matters than traditional views on borderline dynamics. In Kernberg's theory and those derived from it, the origins of splitting are largely nonrelational, and splitting itself becomes something of a brute fact in the psyche. The object relational theory developed here reveals the nexus of relational needs and fears woven into this form of splitting and describes the clinical path to the resolution of these primitive conflicts.)

The making of antidotes for poison and the transformation of poison into real food became central themes in our work from this point on—that is, for another four years. For food to become good, however, intense fears of what Damon thought he would receive from me and what he feared he would do to me had to be worked through. When we eventually accomplished this, Damon was able to internalize something good from me without undue anxiety and to eat food with some degree of comfort.

Damon's fears about what would happen in our relationship were more clearly expressed as we progressed in our antidote work. Nine months into the treatment, I told Damon about an upcoming holiday vacation that would involve our missing several sessions. He immediately began a story about poison water. After deriving comfort from a tale about two superheroes who were buddies and could take on anything, he ended the session by saying, "Help! I live with Skeletor," expressing the horror of living with this bad internal object. In the next session, he was the evil "Iron Man," who tried to trick the man from the Safe Place and kill him—obviously an expression of his anger at me for being an evil trickster who lures children with a promise of help only to abandon them. The man from the Safe Place tried to be sympathetic and suggested that Iron Man was poisoned or under a curse. Iron Man just continued his attacks and said, "I will kill you, or you will have to kill me" three times. The man from the Safe Place asked why he would have to kill Iron Man, and Iron Man said, "Do you want that?" and jammed the man repeatedly with his phallic gun. I would have to kill Damon to protect myself from sexual assault, death, or both. The impossibility of relationship could not be clearer. I would kill him in self-defense, or, killing me, he would deserve to die. Either way he would be both perpetrator and victim.

When I returned from vacation and his fears of abandonment and death were falsified, Damon began to find a way out of his dilemmas. He learned how to lip-synch the Michael Jackson song and video "Thriller," in which a young man protects a young girl who is threatened by monsters. The video ends with Michael Jackson becoming a monster himself. The story clearly demonstrates Damon's wish and fear of becoming an abuser. He was, however, able to use the story as the start of a way out of complete possession by negative internalized models of relating. First, there was a sense of a positive identification with Michael Jackson—his abilities, success, and popularity. As Damon would lip-synch the song, session after session, I was the admiring photographer and audience who applauded everything about him. Michael Jackson's helping the girl seemed to mean something to Damon as well, even though this assistance turns out to be deceptive in the video. Damon also used the video as a way of beginning to demarcate reality and fantasy. He would become immersed in the drama, including Michael's sinister transformation at the end. When our session was over, he would shut off the tape machine, resume his regular identity, and go back to school. I once asked him, with great therapeutic seriousness, how Michael Jackson stopped being a monster. He replied matter-of-factly, "Oh, he takes off his costume and his makeup." (He let me know in the next sessions that it was not quite so simple and that he had heard my serious question:

he created stories about a character with a mask. When the mask was taken away, there was just another mask or a truly monstrous face.)

It was during this time of greater development of a "Michael Jackson" identity (and a somewhat less noticeable identification with me, my orderliness in the office, and my interest in safety) that we began to help sick and injured dinosaurs. X-rays generally revealed damage from anal impregnation. The day after this impregnation was made fully explicit, he told dormitory staff about his father's physical abuse of him and his sister.

This phase of identity consolidation through Michael Jackson and overt identification with me lasted more than three months. As it came to an end, Damon revealed directly how important my tangible presence was in maintaining whatever sense of self, safety, and relatedness he had and in preventing a regression into primitive and agonizing states. As noted earlier, his response to my absences was powerful, often involving themes of death and destruction. But now, some fifteen months into the treatment, when I told him about a long vacation that would start in two weeks, he told me that he lives on an "Island of Pain . . . where it hurts so much even you would scream" or takes refuge in the "Land of Mirrors," which is up in the air. In the Land of Mirrors there is less pain, but one never knows what is real, and everything is broken into kaleidoscopic uncertainty. At times there were frightening things in the mirrors, as when he saw a werewolf. Trapped in this lonely and terrifying place, he would try to smash his way out. He never succeeded.

Damon's transference fears were most explicitly expressed after my return from this vacation. Following considerable discussion with the entire clinical team, I informed him that we would now meet three times a week. He immediately played out a story of a baby's wonderful father who becomes crazed, then violent, then murderous because of "a brain fever." In the next session, he played out a story in which I was a runaway locomotive, and he had to protect the children who were tied to the tracks.

After expressing these transference fears so explicitly, Damon was able to reveal the primitive anxieties at the core of his distress. In the nineteenth and twentieth months of the treatment, he created stories in which babies had to watch unspeakable, unrelenting violence. When my characters protested that this was not right and bad for the babies, the adult characters began to have aggressive and orgiastic sex. The complete inability or unwillingness of parents to shield or protect the children was apparent throughout. The babies were, in fact, brought into the sexual activity. When one of my characters said, "Babies shouldn't have to watch this, either!" Damon broke completely from the story and asked me directly, "You mean really?" He seemed to contemplate my assurance that yes, in reality, babies should not have to watch this. When I suggested a search for good parents who would protect the babies, Damon came up with Popeye and Olive Oyl. But Olive Oyl was much too passive and allowed abuse to occur. Popeye became much too violent in trying to control the abusive adults and wound up attacking first the adults and then the babies himself. I commented on this, but Damon denied that it happened. I continued to point out that it had happened and how upsetting it was to the babies and to Popeye.

Damon then revealed why Popeye is so caught in his violent ways of relating. Damon had often used the imagery of staying out of dangerous waters, of characters at risk for falling over cliffs, and so on. Now he played out how Popeye was at risk for falling into "the 'Pit' . . . a huge hole that is spinning around." We played out the danger and Popeye's fear ten times in a row. My character kept trying to get Popeye out of the Pit. Every time he did so, Popeye became unspeakably violent. If Popeye fell into the Pit at the end of a session, he would die. I stated an obvious interpretation, "So Popeye fights in order to stay alive." Damon then said, "But actually, fighting makes you dead." Faced with this dilemma of death in the Pit or deadening violence on the land, Popeye contemplated suicide. In later sessions, Damon described how the Spinning Pit contained a spider's web that kept Popeye down, and a one-eyed "Octopus" with many arms, and a giant mouth that devoured all. He showed how the Spinning Pit created a "Wild Tornado" that spun Popeye around. Later it was revealed that this Wild Tornado came into being when Popeye had swallowed something that made him crazy or, alternatively, when a tower exploded inside him and he could not get it out. (Together we made drawings of the Pit and the Octopus, which are reproduced as Figures 8–1 and 8–2.)

In this story Damon demonstrates something of great importance for understanding the abused child's attachment to abusive objects, destructive introjects, and perverse models of relationship. As described in

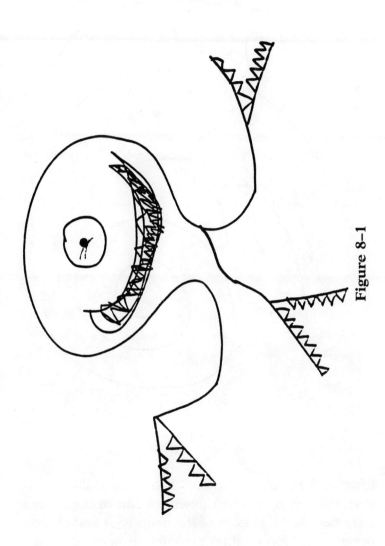

Figure 8–1

Figure 8–2

Chapter 5, negative introjects protect the child against regression into the most powerful and disorganizing anxieties. At the bottom of the dangerous and chaotic ocean of Damon's self lay archaic introjects of the devouring female hole, the polluting phallus, or their fusion in the octopus. To experience these destructive introjects alone is to face psychic annihilation. The child must find some way to stay out of these states, even at the pain of becoming an aggressor or a victim. Identification with the aggressor gives the self some organizing principle and defines a mode of object relationship, albeit intensely conflictual. These monstrous part identities constitute, as Ekstein (1966) says, "transitional introjects" (p. 405), which comfort the child faced with "the anxiety and terror of autistic isolation." The child clings to these negative identity fragments like a drowning person to a raft. To give them up means allowing oneself to sink into the ocean of primordial terror.

The way out of this ultimate dilemma of annihilation anxiety on one side and identification with the aggressor on the other was long and complex. Damon began by documenting the full extent of Popeye's perverseness. Popeye got hold of a baby and beat him up. Then he stepped on the child's ass until the baby shat, and he forced him to eat his own excrement. Popeye masturbated the baby and fondled his anus and then forced the baby to perform fellatio. The wish to beat Popeye up or kill him for abusing the baby was repeatedly manifested in our play, but so was guilt about this wish. Revelation of how evil Popeye was and expression of the baby's wish to kill him seemed to comfort Damon in some way. His play became less frantic and violent, and he began to reveal more about his emotional and physical abuse, to me and to others. In our twenty-first month, Damon introduced another character, "Mask." Mask was "not as bad as Popeye" but was faced with a complex dilemma: he must either kill Popeye, kill himself, be in the Pit, or go to the Land of Mirrors. These, of course, were the impossible choices that confronted Damon. Mask had a friend, "Bonehead," who lived at

the bottom of the ocean. He would die there unless res-
cued, but he derived some nebulous benefit from living there nonetheless. Damon announced that there was
a way out. The heroes would have to work together and
find a way to purify the dangerous medicine that Mask
and Bonehead had found.

In the next several months we did not advance the
story much beyond this point. Instead, the basic facts
and the pain involved were touched on with great vividness, but only from time to time. We would acknowledge how difficult it all is—how Popeye, Mask, or Bonehead had to find some kind of positive identity even
though there seemed to be no way to do this. The
stories continued to express the central need to flee
from psychotic anxieties and isolation into sadomasochistic relationships. But the stories never had quite the
urgency they initially did. Hopes for some kind of good
identity, such as that offered by a superhero, were expressed occasionally, even though we both knew it was
not that simple. Despite the apparent hopelessness of
the situation, neither Damon nor I felt so hopeless. We
both seemed to have the idea that it would just work out,
despite how impossible it seemed. Amazingly, Damon
made significant outward growth during these months
of such troubled play. He began to tolerate physical
contact with me and at times reached out to protect me
from real or imagined dangers in the office or on the
playground. We slowly began to use some of our sessions for playing football, during which he was quite
related, physically vigorous, and not bizarre in his associations. He alluded to my role in his life and began to
talk about where he might go when he left the hospital.

This period of the revelation of basic fears and the

partial attainment of less anxiety-ridden forms of relatedness lasted for several months. As it ended, Damon and I returned to the problem of Mask's medicine, and Damon was able to express transferential fears with ever greater clarity. It was through attention to these transference concerns in the tangible form of medicine that Damon began to progress in more substantive ways toward coping with primordial anxieties and the development of a positive identity. Around the 200th session (about two years into the treatment), we were dealing with Count Dracula, who was alternatively a superhero fighting to preserve himself against attack or the familiar bloodsucker with the added twist that he literally fell to pieces. When I suggested that he never had a normal moment, a normal day, because he was fighting or falling apart, Damon said, with great conviction and seriousness, "He never has a real moment." We demonstrated this in the play several times, that all he has is fighting or falling apart. Damon then said, "Do you want him to live?" I said, "Yes." Damon then brought Dracula over to me, literally in pieces. As I began to put him together, Damon said, "Oh, forget about him." I would not, and I put him back together. Damon then began a story about the good Mighty Mouse and bad Count Dracula. The two, it came out, were essentially linked, were virtually one person. If one of them dies, so does the other. Forgetting about Count Dracula, letting him die, would thus not work: Mighty Mouse would die, too. I said, "Maybe there's a way for the Count to get good without being killed." Damon then wanted to tell me a secret: he had been upset that his great-grandmother had died and that when he thinks about her death he sometimes acts up.

This sequence poignantly reveals the relationship between the splitting of good and bad components of the self and transferential fears of rejection and how even the partial working through of these issues can bring about emotional growth. Damon could integrate the "bad," split-off parts of himself (the destructive oral aggression of Count Dracula) only when he saw that I could accept this "bad self." My acceptance of the whole of him, even the bad, was of central importance in his being able to diminish the split between Dracula and Mighty Mouse and accept himself. This acceptance flew in the face of the powerful transferential fear that I would be repulsed by this bad Count Dracula side and reject Damon. I think Damon sensed that I understood how Dracula represented Damon's intense early needs and his angry response to deprivation and abuse. When Damon saw that I would not leave Count Dracula in pieces, that I wanted him to live, and that I could imagine his becoming good, Damon could begin to accept the needy and rageful parts of himself. With this came a small but real recognition of sadness around his great-grandmother's death and the capacity to see the connection between this event, his feelings, and his acting out. The capacity to bear depressive affect began when the fears of rejection of the bad self and consequent splitting were partially worked through.

After the pivotal session just discussed, Damon would often ask if I liked or accepted his various characters. At the same time, we were able to readdress the issues of object hunger—but this time with much *less* fear of poisoning or violation. In the 210th session, Damon wore my winter boots, tried to walk like me, and in general tried to be just like me. Then his "Goofy"

character became a scientist w ho tried to turn poisons
into good things. He was, however, thinking of giving
up in hopelessness. We talked of how sad this was. I
wondered if we might not be able to turn the poison into
food. Damon said, "Goofy is so hungry he's going to
die." The feeling of sadness was palpable between us. I
gave Damon some of the crackers I had brought for my
lunch. Then Goofy died and dripped away, becoming
just a puddle on the floor. There was nothing left but
his hat. "He can't feel a thing," Damon said. Sadness
gripped us both again, and we munched on our crackers. In each of the remaining 204 sessions of the treatment, we had cookies, crackers, or special snacks. In
our following session, Damon was able to keep the "tea"
he made at the sink and the poison more separate. He
suddenly asked, "Do you like Goofy?" Of course, I said,
"Yes." "Would you like Goofy if he did something bad?"
Again, I said, "Yes." "If he kicked your picture?" I said
I would be mad about the picture but would still like
him. "And if they took me to a hospital?" "Yes," I replied. Damon then said, "Then I could read the papers,
. . . be a therapist." At the end of this session, Damon
held my hand for the first time.

It was shortly after this that I gave Damon a Polaroid
camera for us to use in our sessions and for him to take
when he left. We began to construct a photograph al-
bum of our work and the treatment center. Many of his
first pictures, taken two years and one month into the
treatment, were of me. Or rather, the pictures were of
different parts of my body taken at somewhat odd
angles. I asked whether someday there would be a picture of the whole of me. He said, with no prompting
from me, "Sure. Then you'll be cured." Damon's stories

now began to take on a more positive cast, with two superheroes joining forces to protect the weak. Together, we brought a spaceship back to "Home, Sweet Home." Anxieties about paternal origins and identifications were expressed in the much more organized form of the " Star Wars" story, in which young Luke must come to terms with the fact that the man who raised him is not his father and that his real father is the evil Darth Vader (the dark father). Damon regularly used various toys in play to mimic the light swords that are so much a part of the Star Wars saga. One day in the thirtieth month of treatment, he used a light sword to practice his baseball swing, and from that point on a comfortable interest in sports, sports heroes, and his own achievements often replaced fantasy play.

Damon and I then began to play football and baseball for sessions on end, with considerable comfort and ease on both of our parts. In general, our relationship was a more "ordinary" one, like father and son or uncle and nephew, and other people at the hospital commented on it. Damon could now express despair and hopelessness about life and cure quite openly, and even some hope as well. He became much more comfortable with eating. His appetite and enjoyment of food both became strong, and we had to carry cookies and crackers on all our expeditions. Damon became much more openly expressive of fear, disappointment, and anger during my vacations and absences, saying before one of them, "Don't leave me alone." (He could, of course, also become anxious and disorganized around the same events, deteriorating into primitive fantasies of skulls and poisons.)

Damon's progress had by now made possible the idea of transition to a less restrictive treatment facility. At exactly three years into the treatment, the treatment team decided he should slowly be prepared for transition. Damon was told that at some point within the foreseeable future, he would be leaving and we would be ending our work. His immediate response was to ask what he would eat after he left, and he said he wanted to "eat the whole ward" (his residential unit). At around the same time, he began to attend a group for boys who had been abused, though his anxiety prevented much productive participation. In our sessions a month later, Damon began to play out witnessing a man sexually assault a girl. Interestingly, I had been meeting privately with his mother for some months. She had decided to enter a kind of parent guidance treatment with me, to help Damon, to facilitate his transition to a treatment setting closer to her home, and to acknowledge what had happened in her life and the lives of her children. (For reasons no one could explain, her daughter, Damon's sister, never had overt or serious emotional problems and seemed to make due with several courses of short-term treatment.) We had decided that Damon should join some of our meetings and that his mother would inform him about the facts of the abuse as she knew them. We announced this plan to him just when he began the stories of witnessing abuse. When she discussed the abuse of his sister with him, Damon listened politely but firmly said that he had not witnessed any abuse by his father. His attitude was one of bafflement and tolerance of us, as though he were saying, "I have no idea what you're talking about, but I'm willing to sit here and listen, for I tend to believe and trust you folks."

The recognition that termination was on the horizon, the explicit attention to abuse as a real event, and the group therapy appeared to focus our work on revelations in dramatic play about the abuse he had witnessed. We began a long sequence of sessions in which he would take me into a dark shower stall, from which, in terror, we would observe a man sexually assault a young girl. The first time we did this, Damon told me, "I want to be a murderer when I grow up." (This comment, like many similar ones, convinced me yet again of how naive are notions that therapy progresses in some kind of linear fashion and how pernicious possession by the bad object can be in the life of the abused boy.) Over the next months, we played out with ever increasing vividness the witnessing of these events, Damon's fear and horror, and then his defense of his father when the police took him away in handcuffs. He portrayed fears of becoming a Freddie Krueger character, told me of dreams that reflected anxiety about aggression, and asked for my help about being shown scary movies. He could now talk openly about how he would miss me when he left. He also asked me where babies come from, and other quite appropriate sex education questions. He began to show more direct curiosity about me, as revealed in questions such as whether I had ever made love to anyone or witnessed a rape. He was finally able to play out his feelings of sexual and aggressive arousal about the scenes in the shower room. After this, he moved quickly to stories in which the man was arrested (but not killed) for "sexual abuse" and for exposing Damon to such scary things. Stopping the abuse became a far more important element in the play. Damon said he would never rape anyone. From time to time I would ask Damon if anything like this had happened to him in real life. He always said no, but often with little conviction. In the midst of yet another session in the shower, just weeks before he was to leave, I said to him, "You don't remember abuse, but you act as if you do." He said, "I know." A week later, as we discussed his leaving and what he would remember of his stay at the hospital, he said that the most important memory he had in his treatment was "about the abuse." When he told his therapy group that he had witnessed sexual abuse, he came to our session and said he was so hungry he wanted to eat "everything." The partial integration of this memory of his sister's abuse allowed for a less conflicted desire about taking in and remembering the people he was now leaving. Memory had (partially) replaced traumatic reliving, and the potential for the internalization of good persons and relationships was established. As the actual termination drew near, Damon frequently expressed the desire to "eat the whole ward." He was outwardly more comfortable with food, with himself, and with expressing his feelings. There were actually a few times when he was spontaneous and unguarded, and he said good-bye with warmth as well as fear.

Damon has recently completed five years of residential treatment during which he received continued intensive psychotherapy. I was able to visit with him twice a year during his residential treatment. He is now a somewhat shy 16-year-old adolescent who likes routine and structure, who is quite comfortable with sports and the aggression in them. Phobic anxiety (for example, around bees) and a certain amount of constriction have replaced the panic and paranoid explosions of his earlier years. He has little or no memory of the overt work that was done in our therapy and group treatment on sexual abuse themes. He has never engaged in sexual acting out of any sort with other children or adults. When his mother gave birth to a half-sister, Damon was quite nurturant and caring of the little girl. Damon identifies his temper and swearing as his main problems. He has been able to articulate feelings of sadness to his current therapist, as well as feelings of weariness and pain about the chronicity of his problems. Damon hopes to become a construction worker when he grows up, for he realizes that his hope of becoming a professional athlete is unrealistic.

Two years or so after ending treatment with me, I asked Damon what he remembered most about our work, and he said, "The Safe Place, that little dish."

9

SUMMARY

In this book, I have attempted to articulate typical but important dynamics that occur in boys who have suffered traumatic neglect and abuse, to embed these dynamics in a theoretical context, and to explain how some of the existing theories about seriously disturbed children have inherent difficulties conceptualizing interpersonal trauma. I have further tried to show how these core dynamics typically manifest themselves in treatment situations, to suggest some perspectives on technique that address the child's relational dilemmas, and to describe a long-term treatment in which the working through of transferential concerns played a pivotal role.

The relational dynamics that hold sway over the abused child are reflected in deeply held beliefs that the child evolves in order to comprehend the suffering and distorted relationships he has had to endure. To cope with the vulnerability and terror of his situation, the abused child typically comes to believe that he caused the abuse and deserved it as well. Male children in particular also defend against powerlessness and vulnerability through identification with the aggressor. This defense provides only the most temporary of respites, for it carries in its wake the dread of doing to others what was done to oneself and immense guilt for any impulse or act in the aggressor role. The horror of these dilemmas is compounded by the child's conviction that the only way to have love is through abuse. The child's object hunger is transformed by the confusion of tongues: the wish for contact is experienced as the wish for a violent or sexual relationship that would be retraumatizing. The child then starves in the midst of poisonous objects: longing to internalize, but afraid that he will internalize something toxic. The search for relatedness in ways that repeat the abusive relationship, painful as it is for the child, serves to protect the child from falling into archaic anxieties. Sadomasochistic relationships serve to prevent regression to an objectless state of total isolation and exposure to the most primitive and disorganizing fears.

Many of the parts of this complex psychological constellation have been described by other clinicians and researchers. There is, however, a value in seeing them all together. If there is anything new in what I have said, it is that identification with the aggressor and the repetition of abusive relationships are held to so strongly because these form a defense against a more or less complete disorganization of the psyche. The child feels in the depths of himself that possession by the bad self, no matter how horrible this is, is preferable to a state of complete psychic disintegration.

The presence of such a powerful anxiety makes integration and transformation of the negative introjects that encode the child's experience of early, abusive relationships difficult. Therapy for such children requires that the negative introjects be metabolized, not expelled or destroyed as the child may wish. The therapeutic process of metabolization requires that the therapist actively enter into this negative domain and eventually interpret the child's transferential fears and longings. The child patient will likely believe that he is going to bring about a mutual possession by bad introjects and re-create the original, traumatic relationships or that the therapist is going to abandon him. Even the partial working through of identification with the negative object and the acute fears of countertransference enactment can allow the child to give up the identification and integrate conflictual feelings of powerlessness, vulnerability, fear, and longing. Greater integration of the split-off bad self overcomes a basic and rigid form of splitting, and it thus allows for the tolerance of depression and the possibility of internalization of good objects.

The agonizing choice the child faces, between identification with the aggressor and annihilation anxiety, requires treatment in which containment allows for the regression he must make to primitive anxieties. When this occurs, a child can come to a new stance toward himself and others and can internalize something good from the therapist. When the child can find a safe place and a place of nurturance with another person and inside himself, a significant change has been brought about. Reasonable hope for the child's future is then a possibility.

APPENDIX:
CONTRAINDICATIONS

It is often asked under what conditions lengthy, in-depth treatment of disturbed and traumatized children should be attempted. In the current social and economic climate, institutional realities often prevent intensive treatment from occurring at all, rendering the clinical questions moot. When, however, adequate treatment is supported, difficult questions still remain as to whether and under what circumstances it is clinically advisable. It is often unclear when psychotherapy of this sort will work and which children will most likely benefit from it. Often, one must simply try and hope for the best. It is easier to define conditions that tend to preclude successful treatment than it is to define conditions that, if met, will assure success. Factors that, in my experience, tend to prevent or diminish the effectiveness of treatment are complex and varied. One group involves characteristics of the child: low IQ, compromised interpersonal and emotional skills, the inability to use fantasy or other affectively rich means of communication, emotional blunting or extreme defensive retreat, and organized sociopathic personality formation all work against engagement in and utilization of the therapeutic relationship. (The capacity to engage deeply and affectively with the therapist is, I believe, of greater import than intelligence as measured by standard tests.) Another cluster concerns the containment of the child: the child must feel safe enough and held enough not only in the sessions themselves but in his or her daily life to engage in a treatment of this sort. Any sort of ongoing abuse or neglect will inevitably unravel the treatment. Addressing previous abuse in some kind of "real" way, such as by using the legal system or family meetings, is often essential. (In my experience, addressing these issues is far more important than successful resolution, whatever that may be understood to be.) In addition, the child must feel psychologically safe enough to engage in a therapy that involves questioning basic assumptions about life, relationship, and psychic integrity. Some significant degree of emotional understanding and behavioral containment by those adults who care for the child is obviously essential. As the child deinternalizes various pathogenic patterns of relatedness, the caretaking adults must recognize that this is a step forward, however difficult it may be in the practical moment. The child must feel fundamentally supported by parents or the adults in the parental role, who must also validate the treatment process. Family and group treatment are often essential. With children as disturbed as the boys described here, residential treatment is typically a necessity not only for substantive treatment but also for the child's basic safety and containment.

The therapist also must feel supported and contained by the institutional setting of the therapy. He or she must feel safe with the child and with the primitive issues evoked by the treatment. The therapist needs to feel respected and supported by colleagues. One important aspect of support is adequate supervision. In the therapeutic relationship itself, there must be sufficient basic human warmth. No matter how intense the work, there must not be undue countertransferential sadism, inhibition, or remoteness. Seriously traumatized children will feel despair, anger, and confusion when confronted with therapists who are "nice" but who fail to recognize the extent of the pain the child feels and the power of identification with the aggressor and who, as a result, fail to grapple actively with the child's negative internal objects.

It should be obvious that the therapeutic relationship must be long enough and frequent enough to support the child's psyche in such difficult work. Reconstructive treatment of psyches so damaged can take years and require multiple meetings per week. One of the most painful and difficult things for a clinician is the recognition that a child needs and is ready to participate in a substantive treatment when this form of therapy cannot be offered because of economic or institutional constraints. While there is no substitute for substantive treatment, children can benefit from a less rigorous therapy in which the ultimate depths of the child's agony are hinted at rather than exposed, mentioned rather than worked through. The child can derive significant benefit from feeling that the therapist understands what the ultimate concerns actually are and that this understanding informs the therapist's responses to the child. Under these conditions, some children can absorb a good deal from the therapist's personality and grow in a way that is not entirely artificial. The more disturbed parts of the child's personality may slowly retreat, in a process rather like the reclaiming of land from the sea.

It is one of the more painful ironies of contemporary therapeutic practice that at the very time we are learning so much about the healing power of relationship, our institutions and ideologies so often prevent these relationships from occurring. Much of the time, our public mental health system pursues policies that encourage fragmented, incomplete, and ultimately cruel treatment in which the basic anxieties and needs of the traumatized child are not addressed. If this book has any direct social utility, it is as a demonstration that only through relationship is trauma in relationship cured.

REFERENCES

Ainsworth, M. D. S. (1982). Attachment: retrospect and prospect. In *The Place of Attachment in Human Behavior*, ed. C. M. Parkes and J. Stevenson-Hinde, pp. 3–30. New York: Basic Books.

Ainsworth, M. D. S., Blehar, M. C., Waters, E., and Wall, S. (1978). *Patterns of Attachment: A Psychological Study of the Strange Situation*. Hillsdale, NJ: Erlbaum.

Balint, M. (1979). *The Basic Fault: Therapeutic Aspects of Regression*. New York: Brunner/Mazel. (Reprint of the 1969 publication by Tavistock, London.)

Berliner, B. (1958). The role of object relations in moral masochism. *Psychoanalytic Quarterly* 27:38–56.

Bion, W. R. (1959). Attacks on linking. *International Journal of Psycho-Analysis* 40:5–6.

Blos, P. (1971). Adolescent concretization. In *Currents in Psychoanalysis*, ed. I. M. Marcus, pp. 66–88. New York:

International Universities Press. (Reprinted in *The Adolescent Passage: Developmental Issues*, ed. P. Blos. New York: International Universities Press, 1979.)

Bowlby, J. (1969). *Attachment and Loss: Attachment*, vol. 1. New York: Basic Books.

———— (1973). *Attachment and Loss: Separation*, vol. 2. New York: Basic Books.

———— (1980). *Attachment and Loss: Loss, Sadness, and Depression*, vol. 3. New York: Basic Books.

———— (1988). *A Secure Base: Clinical Applications of Attachment Theory*. London: Routledge & Kegan Paul.

Bretherton, I. (1985). Attachment theory: retrospect and prospect. In *Growing Points of Attachment Theory and Research*, ed. I. Bretherton and E. Waters, *Monographs of the Society for Research in Child Development* 50(1–2): 3–35, Serial No. 209.

Briere, J. (1989). *Therapy for Adults Molested as Children*. New York: Springer.

Browne, A., and Finkelhor, D. (1986). Impact of child sexual abuse: a review of the research. *Psychological Bulletin* 99:66–77.

Carmen, E. H., Rieker, P. P., and Mills, T. (1984). Victims of violence and psychiatric illness. *American Journal of Psychiatry* 141:378–383.

Coons, P. M. (1986). Psychiatric problems associated with child abuse: a review. In *Psychiatric Sequelae of Child Abuse*, ed. J. Jacobson, pp. 169–200. Springfield, Ill.: Charles C Thomas.

Davies, J. M., and Frawley, M. G. (1992). Dissociative processes and transference–countertransference paradigms in the psychoanalytically oriented treatment of adult survivors of childhood sexual abuse. *Psychoanalytic Dialogue* 2(1):5–36.

DeLozier, P. P. (1982). Attachment theory and child abuse. In *The Place of Attachment in Human Behavior*, ed.

C. M. Parkes and J. Stevensen-Hinde, pp. 95–117. New York: Basic Books.

Ekstein, R. (1966). *Children of Time and Space, of Action and Impulse.* New York: Jason Aronson. (Reprinted in 1983.)

Emslie, G. T., and Rosenfeld, A. A. (1983). Incest reported by children and adolescents hospitalized for severe psychiatric problems. *American Journal of Psychiatry* 140:708–711.

Eth, S., and Pynoos, R. S. (1985). Developmental perspective on psychic trauma in childhood. In *Trauma and Its Wake: The Study of Treatment of Post-Traumatic Stress Disorders,* ed. C. Figley, pp. 36–52. New York: Brunner/Mazel.

Fairbairn, W. R. D. (1952). The repression and return of bad objects. In *An Object-Relations Theory of the Personality,* ed. W. R. D. Fairbairn, pp. 102–126. New York: Basic Books.

Fast, I., and Chethik, M. (1972). Some aspects of object relations in borderline children. *International Journal of Psycho-Analysis* 53(4):479–485.

Ferenczi, S. (1933). Confusion of tongues between adults and the child: the language of tenderness and of passion. In *Final Contributions to the Problems and Methods of Psycho-analysis,* ed. M. Balint, pp. 156–167. New York: Brunner/Mazel, 1955.

Finkelhor, D. (1979). *Sexually Victimized Children.* New York: Free Press.

——— (1987). The sexual abuse of children: current research reviewed. *Psychiatric Annals: The Journal of Continuing Psychiatric Education* 17(4):233–241.

Finkelhor, D., and Browne, A. (1985). The traumatic impact of child sexual abuse: a conceptualization. *American Journal of Orthopsychiatry* 55(4):530–541.

Freud, S. (1920). Beyond the pleasure principle. *Standard Edition* 18:3–66.

—— (1923). The ego and the id. *Standard Edition* 19:3–66.

—— (1926). Inhibitions, symptoms and anxiety. *Standard Edition* 20:77–175.

—— (1940). An outline of psycho-analysis. *Standard Edition* 23:141–207.

Geleerd, E. R. (1958). Borderline states in childhood and adolescence. *Journal of the American Psychoanalytic Association* 2:279–295.

Gianino, A., and Tronick, E. (1988). The mutual regulation model: the infant's self and interactive regulation and coping and defensive capacities. In *Stress and Coping*, ed. R. Field, P. McCabe, and N. Schneiderman, pp. 47–68. Hillsdale, NJ: Erlbaum.

Goodwin, J. M. (1990). Applying to adult victims what we have learned from children. In *Incest-Related Syndromes of Adult Pathology*, ed. R. P. Kluft, pp. 55–75. Washington, DC: American Psychiatric Press.

Goodwin, J. M., Cheever, K., and Cornell, V. (1990). Borderline and other severe symptoms in adult survivors of incestuous abuse. *Psychiatric Annals* 20(1):22–32.

Green, A. H. (1978). Psychopathology of abused children. *Journal of the American Academy of Child Psychiatry* 17:92–103.

—— (1983). Dimensions of psychological trauma in abused children. *Journal of the American Academy of Child Psychiatry* 22(3):231–237.

Greenberg, J. R., and Mitchell, S. A. (1983). *Object Relations in Psychoanalytic Theory*. Cambridge, MA: Harvard University Press.

Greenman, D. A., Gunderson, J. G., Cane, M., and Saltzman, P. R. (1986). An examination of the borderline diagnosis in children. *American Journal of Psychiatry* 143:998–1003.

Herman, J. L. (1981). *Father–Daughter Incest*. Cambridge, MA: Harvard University Press.

—— (1992). *Trauma and Recovery.* New York: Basic Books.

Herman, J. L., Perry, J. C., and van der Kolk, B. A. (1989). Childhood trauma in borderline personality disorder. *American Journal of Psychiatry* 146:490–495.

Hopkins, J. (1984). The probable role of trauma in a case of foot and shoe fetishism: aspects of the psychotherapy of a 6-year-old-girl. *International Review of Psycho-Analysis* 11:79.

—— (1986). Solving the mystery of monsters: steps towards the recovery from trauma. *Journal of Child Psychotherapy* 12(1):61.

James, D. (1989). *Treating Traumatized Children: New Insights and Creative Interventions.* Lexington, MA: Lexington Books.

Jones, D. P. (1986). Individual psychotherapy for the sexually abused child. *Child Abuse and Neglect* 10:377–385.

Kelmpe, C. H., and Helfer, R. E. (1968). *The Battered Child.* Chicago: University of Chicago Press.

Kernberg, O. (1966). Structural derivatives of object relations. *International Journal of Psycho-Analysis* 47:236.

—— (1976). *Object Relations and Clinical Psychoanalysis.* New York: Jason Aronson.

Kernberg, P. (1983). Borderline conditions: childhood and adolescent aspects. In *The Borderline Child: Approaches to Etiology, Diagnosis, and Treatment,* ed. K. S. Robson, pp. 102–119. New York: McGraw-Hill.

Kestenbaum, C. (1983). The borderline child at risk for major psychiatric disorder in adult life: seven case reports with follow-up. In *The Borderline Child: Approaches to Etiology, Diagnosis, and Treatment,* ed. K. S. Robson, pp. 49–81. New York: McGraw-Hill.

Kluft, R. P. (1984). Multiple personality in childhood. *Psychiatric Clinics of North America* 7(1):121–134.

——, ed. (1985). *Childhood Antecedents of Multiple Personality.* Washington, DC: American Psychiatric Press.

Knight, R. P. (1953). Borderline states. *Bulletin of the Menninger Clinic* 17(1):1–12.

Levine, H. B. (1990). *Adult Analysis and Childhood Sexual Abuse.* Hillsdale, NJ: Erlbaum.

Lofgren, D. P., Bemporad, J., King, J., et al. (1991). A prospective follow-up study of so-called borderline children. *American Journal of Psychiatry* 148(11):1541–1547.

Lyons-Ruth, K. (1991). Rapprochement as approachment: Mahler's theory reconsidered from the vantage point of recent research on early attachment relationships. *Psychoanalytic Psychology* 8(1):1–23.

Lyons-Ruth, K., Connell, D., and Zoll, D. (1989). Patterns of maternal behavior among infants at risk for abuse: relations with infant attachment behavior and infant development at 12 months of age. In *Child Maltreatment: Theory and Research on the Causes and Consequences of Child Abuse and Neglect,* ed. D. Cicchetti and V. Carlson, pp. 464–493. New York: Cambridge University Press.

Mahler, M. S. (1971). A study of the separation-individuation process and its possible application to borderline phenomena in the psychoanalytic situation. *Psychoanalytic Study of the Child* 26:403–424.

Mahler, M., Pine, F., and Bergman, A. (1975). *The Psychological Birth of the Human Infant.* New York: Basic Books.

Main, M., and Cassidy, J. (1988). Categories of response to reunion with the parent at age six: predicted from infant attachment classifications and stable over a one-month period. *Developmental Psychology* 24(3):415–426.

Main, M., and Hesse, E. (1990). Parents' unresolved traumatic experiences are related to infant disorganized status: Is frightened and/or frightening parental behavior the linking mechanism? In *Attachment in the Preschool Years,* ed. M. Greenberg, D. Cicchetti, and M. Cummings, pp. 161–184. Chicago: University of Chicago Press.

References

181

Main, M., Kaplan, N., and Cassidy, J. (1985). Security of attachment in infancy, childhood, and adulthood: a move to the level of representation. In *Growing Points in Attachment Theory and Research*, ed. I. Bretherton and E. Waters. *Society for Research in Child Development Monographs* 49(6):198, Serial No. 209.

Main, M., and Weston, D. (1981). Security of attachment to mother and father: related to conflict. *Child Development* 52:932–940.

Masson, J. (1984). *The Assault on Truth: Freud's Suppression of the Seduction Theory*. New York: Farrar, Straus & Giroux.

Masterson, J. F. (1972). *Treatment of the Borderline Adolescent: A Developmental Approach*. New York: Wiley.

Miller, A. (1981). *Prisoners of Childhood*. New York: Basic Books.

——— (1983). *For Your Own Good*. New York: Farrar, Straus & Giroux.

Parsons, E. A. (1991). *Maternal behavior and disorganized attachment: relational sequelae of traumatic experience*. Unpublished doctoral dissertation, Massachusetts School of Professional Psychology, Dedham, MA.

Perry, J. C., Herman, J. L., van der Kolk, B. A., and Hoke, L. A. (1990). Psychotherapy and psychological trauma in borderline personality disorder. *Psychiatric Annals* 20(1):33–43.

Pine, F. (1974). On the concept "Borderline" in children: a clinical essay. *The Psychoanalytic Study of the Child* 29:341–368.

——— (1986). On the development of the "borderline-child-to-be." *American Journal of Orthopsychiatry* 56(3):450–457.

Putnam, F. W., Guroff, J. J., Silberman, E. K., et al. (1986). The clinical phenomenology of multiple personality disorder: review of 100 recent cases. *Journal of Clinical Psychiatry* 47:6.

Rinsley, D. B. (1978). Borderline psychopathology: a review of aetiology, diagnosis, and treatment. *International Review of Psycho-Analysis* 5:45–54.

———— (1980). Diagnosis and treatment of borderline children and adolescents. *Bulletin of the Menninger Clinic* 44(2):147–170.

———— (1985). Notes on the pathogenesis and nosology of borderline and narcissistic personality disorders. *Journal of the American Academy of Psychoanalysis* 13:317–328.

Rosenfeld, S. K., and Sprince, M. P. (1963). An attempt to formulate the meaning of the concept "borderline." *Psychoanalytic Study of the Child* 18:603–635. New York: International Universities Press.

———— (1965). Some thoughts on the technical handling of borderline children. *The Psychoanalytic Study of the Child* 20:495–516.

Saunders, E. A., and Arnold, F. (1993). A critique of conceptual and treatment approaches to borderline psychopathology in light of findings about childhood abuse. *Psychiatry* 56:188–202.

Schetky, D. H. (1990). A review of the literature on the long-term effects of childhood sexual abuse. In *Incest-Related Syndromes of Adult Pathology*, ed. R. P. Kluft, pp. 35–54. Washington, DC: American Psychiatric Press.

Sgroi, S. M. (1982). *A Handbook of Clinical Intervention in Child Sexual Abuse*. Lexington, MA: Lexington Books.

Shapiro, T. (1983). The borderline syndrome in children: a critique. In *The Borderline Child: Approaches to Etiology, Diagnosis, and Treatment*, ed. K. S. Robson, pp. 12–29. New York: McGraw-Hill.

Shengold, L. (1989). *Soul Murder: The Effects of Childhood Abuse and Deprivation*. New Haven, CT: Yale University Press.

Smith, H. F., Bemporad, J. R., and Hanson, G. (1982). Aspects of the treatment of borderline children. *American Journal of Psychotherapy* 36(2):181–197.

Smith, S., ed. (1978). *The Maltreatment of Children.* Baltimore, MD: University Park Press.

Sroufe, L. A., and Fleeson, J. (1986). Attachment and the construction of relationships. In *The Nature and Development of Relationship,* ed. W. W. Hartup and Z. Rubin. New York: Erlbaum.

Stern, D. N. (1985). *The Interpersonal World of the Infant.* New York: Basic Books.

Summit, R., and Kryso, J. (1978). Sexual abuse of children: a clinical spectrum. *American Journal of Orthopsychiatry* 48(2):237–251.

Terr, L. C. (1991). Childhood traumas: an outline and overview. *American Journal of Psychiatry* 148(1):10–20.

Tronick, E., and Gianino, A. (1986). The transmission of maternal disturbance to the infant. In *New Directions for Child Development: Maternal Depression and Infant Disturbance,* vol. 34, ed. E. Tronick and T. Field, pp. 5–11. San Francisco: Jossey-Bass.

Ulman, R., and Brothers, D. (1988). *A Psychoanalytic Study of Trauma: The Shattered Self.* Hillsdale, NJ: Analytic Press.

Valenstein, A. F. (1973). On attachment to painful feelings and the negative therapeutic reaction. In *Psychoanalytic Study of the Child.* vol. 28, pp. 365–392. New Haven, CT: Yale University Press.

van der Kolk, B., ed. (1987). *Psychological Trauma.* Washington, DC: American Psychiatric Press.

Walker, L. E. A., and Bolkovatz, M. A. (1988). Play therapy with children who have experienced sexual assault. In *Handbook on Sexual Abuse of Children: Assessment and Treatment Issues,* ed. L. E. A. Walker, pp. 249–269. New York: Springer.

Winnicott, D. W. (1962). Ego integration in child development. In *The Maturational Processes and the Facilitating Environment: Studies in the Theory of Emotional Development,* pp. 56–63. New York: International Universities Press.

Zanarini, M. C., Gunderson, J. G., Marino, M. F., et al. (1989). Childhood experiences of borderline patients. *Comprehensive Psychiatry* 30(1):18–25.

Zeanah, C. H., and Zeanah, P. D. (1989). Intergenerational transmission of maltreatment: insights from attachment theory and research. *Psychiatry* 52(May):177–196.

INDEX